Microwave Cooking · Holidays & Parties

Litton Microwave Cooking Products, Minneapolis, Minnesota

CERTIFIED FOR MICROWAVE COOKING

LITTON Microwave Cooking Products

CREDITS:

Design and Production: Cy DeCosse Creative Department, Inc.
Author: Barbara Methven
Art Directors: Stuart Smith, Eugene Buck
Production Coordinators: Julia Slott, Christine Watkins, Bonita Machel, Elizabeth Woods
Photographers: Michael Jensen, Buck Holzemer, Ken Greer
Food Stylists: Suzanne Finley, Carol Grones, Lynn Lohmann, Maria Rolandelli, Susan Zechmann
Home Economists: Jill Crum, Peggy Lamb, Maureen Mortinson, Susan Zechmann
Typesetting: Jennie Smith
Color Separations: Weston Engraving Co., Inc.
Printing: Moebius Printing Co.

This is no ordinary recipe book. It's like a cooking school in your home, ready to answer questions on the spot. Step-by-step photographs show you how to prepare food for microwaving, what to do during cooking, how to tell when the food is done. A new photo technique shows you how foods look during microwaving.

The foods selected for this book are basic in several ways. All microwave well and demonstrate the advantages of microwaving. They are popular foods you prepare frequently, so the book will be useful in day-to-day cooking. Each food illustrates a principle or technique of microwaving which you can apply to similar recipes you find in magazines or other cookbooks.

This book was designed to obtain good results in all brands of ovens. Techniques may vary from the cookbook developed for your oven. If rotating foods is unnecessary in your oven, that technique may be eliminated. All foods are cooked at either High or 50% power (Medium). The Defrost setting on earlier ovens and Simmer setting on current ovens may be used when Medium is called for. This simplifies the choice of settings while you become familiar with the reasons why different foods require different power levels.

Microwaving is easy as well as fast. The skills you develop with this book will help you make full and confident use of your microwave oven.

The Litton Microwave Cooking Center

Contents

What You Need to Know Before You Start

Styles in entertaining change, but parties are as popular as ever. Most parties today are more casual than the formal and elaborate entertaining style of the past. Many of us do not have the leisure time to cook such meals and our guests often prefer lighter fare. Today's successful party respects lighter eating habits, offering sensible portions of food, appetizing and attractively presented.

The microwave oven fits this contemporary style. It allows you to cook food quickly. Many dishes can be prepared in advance and reheated without loss of flavor or quality. You can freeze foods to defrost and reheat just before serving. The microwave oven cuts cooking time so you enjoy the party.

Whether you are planning a special occasion party or just a simple gathering of friends, this book will help you utilize your microwave oven to its optimum. From the 31 menu ideas presented, you can prepare a buffet for 20 guests or a romantic Valentine's Day dinner for two. There are American favorites for traditional holidays and exotic foreign foods to lend more variety to your entertaining.

Each menu includes step-by-step preparation information to help you manage your time, special hints on table settings and serving suggestions to make your party look as good as it tastes. Recipes for all the foods in the menu section appear in the second half of the book with handy cross-references. You can choose an entire menu or mix and match recipes to suit your own entertaining needs.

Three Types of Parties

Statistics show that most microwave oven owners work outside the home. They enjoy entertaining, but can't devote days to food preparation.

The parties in this book are designed to fit different situations. Choose the ones which suit your schedule. Check the time management box that accompanies each menu to see which of these time categories apply.

Advance preparation parties. Most of the menus allow you to spread the work over several evenings. Foods can be refrigerated or frozen after preparing. When the party day arrives, you're relaxed and most of the food is ready.

One-day parties. Some of the meals are easy enough to be prepared the day of the party. They are festive, but fit today's casual style.

Impromptu parties. An impromptu party is one that happens without notice. With your microwave oven and freezer, you can be ready. Make party foods for the freezer in your spare time. Entrées frozen in two-serving packages are the most convenient size for microwave-freezer use. They freeze and defrost rapidly and evenly, and are more versatile than bulk packages. You can serve as few as two people, or to serve more guests, defrost more packages.

Getting Organized

Each of the parties in this book includes time management for food preparation. For successful, unhurried entertaining, organize your time before cooking by following these steps.

Decide on the number of guests and invite them up to 2 to 3 weeks in advance. Parties pre-pared with the microwave oven are not limited to small groups, but the number of guests determines the type of party you choose. Even when dishes are prepared in advance, more food takes a longer time to reheat, so allow a looser timetable for larger groups.

Space is important. The size of your table limits the number of guests at a seated dinner. A buffet for a larger group can be formal, if you have enough tableware, or casual if you need to use paper plates.

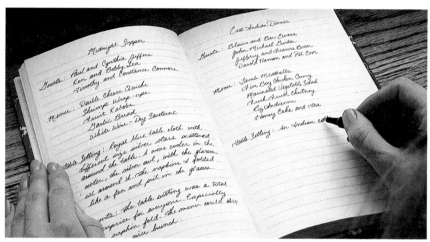

Plan the occasion. Select a menu, a theme for the party and decide whether service will be formal or casual. Keep a party diary in a notebook or on cards in your recipe file. List the guests, menu and table setting. After the party, add your comments. You'll want to repeat your favorite parties, but not for the same guests.

Read through the recipes. Make marketing lists of ingredients needed and check staples to make sure you have enough. Do most shopping ahead of time, leaving only perishables for last-minute shopping.

Choose your table setting. Some party givers devote a cupboard shelf to party equipment. Others use a notebook or card file to jot down ideas for use in the future.

Decide on the table covering and napkins and get them ready. Select a serving dish for each food and the tableware you will use. Fill salt shakers and polish silver or crystal if necessary. Choose a centerpiece. Remember that the food is part of the table decoration. Make a shopping list of things you will need to complete the setting, such as candles, paper products or flowers.

Decorating the Table

Effective presentation turns an ordinary dinner into a party. You don't need special tableware or professional floral arrangements. A touch of surprise and imagination create a memorable setting with everyday materials.

The most important decorative element is the food. Everything else is background for it.

Accent its shape and color with attractive, but not elaborate, garnishes. Try some of the simple techniques on page 12.

Make an inventory of things you have around the house which could vary your table settings. You may never have thought to use them before. Record your ideas in your party diary so

you'll remember when the need arises. Old, one-of-a-kind items from grandmother's attic or a garage sale — like a crystal decanter, a china platter or bowl, or a pair of goblets — can appear as serving dishes, candle holders or centerpieces.

Tablecloths can be made from gaily printed sheets or remnants. For a contemporary look, cover the table with shiny shelf paper, foil or wallpaper.

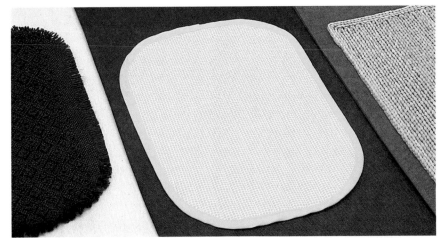

Table mats can be used by themselves; contrasting or printed mats look attractive placed over a solid cloth. If you make your own mats, make them large enough to accommodate the place setting without crowding. A generous mat looks dramatic and protects your table from rings and stains.

Runners are an effective change from table mats, and are easier to make. Cross a pair of runners on a small table for four. On a large table, lay two long runners under the plates, leaving the table bare in the center. For a new look, use runners over a cloth.

Old linens, like dresser scarves, bridge cloths or crocheted doilies can be centered over a plain tablecloth to accent the centerpiece and provide variety.

Flowers should be kept low so guests can see over them. Arrange them yourself in unusual containers, such as a tea pot, gravy boat, or wooden box. Tuck sprigs of baby's breath in liqueur glasses and set one at each place.

Food from the menu, such as a cake, a bowl of fruit, or dishes of nuts and candies can double as a centerpiece. Create a still life of polished vegetables or unusually shaped breads.

Candles should be above or below eye level. Cluster candles of several heights or thicknesses. Secure candles in glasses or shells with florist's clay. Use them with a centerpiece or at each place.

House plants come to the table with their pots tied up in a silk scarf or table napkin. Set them in baskets or cluster them in a shallow baking dish.

Collections add personal interest to the table. Try antique kitchen utensils at a casual meal or porcelain figures at a formal one. Set an arrangement of small boxes or crystal objects on a mirror.

Serving pieces don't have to match the dishes. Oven-to-table microwave cookware helps keep food hot and saves preparation and cleanup time. As an accent, use a plate from another set of dishes, or a bowl you bought on vacation.

Dinnerware can be china, pottery, glass or paper. Contrasting tableware looks very effective in a stacked setting of dinner plate, salad plate and soup bowl.

Setting the Table

A buffet meal is usually served from a table. But you can use any convenient surface which offers enough space for foods, utensils and room for the guests to move as they serve themselves. A side board, bookcase or kitchen counter can serve as a buffet.

Traffic and space are the main considerations in choosing a buffet arrangement. If possible, guests should approach the table from one direction and leave in another, so guests juggling full plates won't need to thread their way through a line.

A buffet moves clockwise. It is arranged in a logical order with space near each serving dish where guests can set down their plates to serve themselves. Plates come first, then the main dish and any sauces or condiments which go with it.

Next are hot accompaniments, like vegetables and rice or potatoes. Salads, relishes, and breads follow.

At a traditional buffet, bread and rolls are buttered in advance. With so many people watching their diets, many hostesses serve plain breads and pats of butter, so guests can decide for themselves.

Once an arrangement is chosen, try it out in advance. Select the serving pieces you

One-line buffet set on a table in the center of the room, allows plenty of space for food and beverage. It's a good choice when your table is small because it uses four sides.

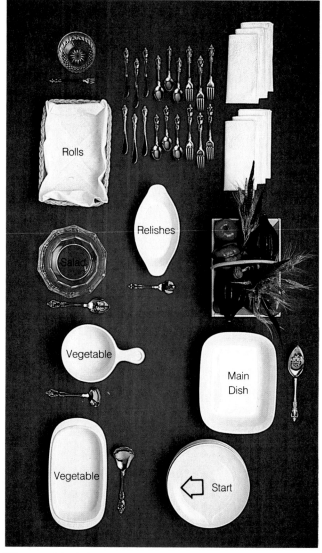

Three-sided buffet is arranged on a table placed against the wall. Use it in a small room to allow more space for traffic. "Centerpiece" is set to the rear of the table. If you don't have room for the beverage, serve it from another table.

will use and set them out to make sure they look good together and suit the space.

After a buffet meal, clear the table and re-set it for dessert. If you prefer, dessert and coffee can be served from a different table or passed on a tray. Provide a place where guests can set used flatware and plates before dessert is served.

For sit-down dinners, table settings are simpler now than they were in grandmother's day.

Elaborate protocol has been replaced by convenience.

Bread plates and butter knives are optional. If salad is served with the main course, you can omit the salad fork, or place it to the left of the dinner fork.

For a soup course, set the spoon at the far right. Soup bowl and underliner can be placed on the dinner plate. For more formality, bring dinner and salad plates to the table after the soup course.

Place setting above is traditional when salad is served before the main course. Arrange flatware in the order of use, with the first items on the outside.

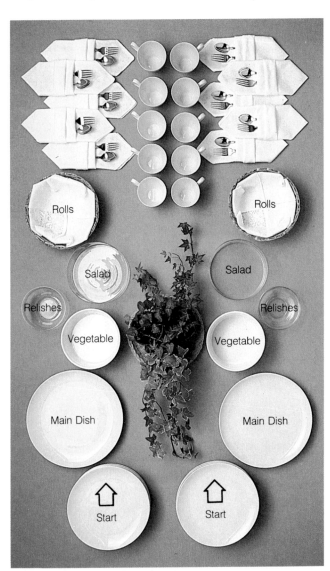

Two-line buffet speeds serving for a large group. Beverage may be served from the end of the table or a separate table. Provide two serving dishes of each food item, so the table is the same on both sides.

Formal tea is a two-line buffet with coffee served at one end and tea at the other. Guests choose the line for the beverage they prefer. Ask two of your friends to pour.

Garnishing

Simple garnishes serve two purposes. They make foods look attractive and festive. Some, like chopped parsley or crumbled bacon, add flavor and texture contrast.

Crisping raw vegetables sets their shape and improves texture and freshness.

Crisping. Place cut-up raw vegetables in bowl of cool water. Cover and refrigerate.

Carrot curls. Peel carrots. With vegetable peeler, cut thin, lengthwise strips. Roll up strips; secure with wooden pick. Crisp.

Fluffy parsley. Chop unwashed parsley. Place in dish towel. Bring ends of towel up to form bag. Hold under cool running water; squeeze dry. Spread parsley on paper towels. Wrap in paper towel and refrigerate up to 3 days.

Radish crysanthemum. Place radish between two chopsticks. Slice down to sticks at ⅛-in. intervals. Rotate 90° and repeat. Crisp.

Fluted mushrooms. Wash, dry and trim mushrooms. Make V-shaped cuts from center to edge of cap. Lift out wedges. For spiral flute, rotate cap against knife while cutting. Refrigerate in plastic bag.

Celery and scallion brushes. Cut vegetables in 3-in. lengths. Slit both ends of celery almost to center in narrow strips. Make 4 or more intersecting cuts in bulb end of scallion. Crisp.

Citrus twist. Thinly slice lemon, lime or orange. Cut the slice, leaving one edge of peel intact. Twist into 'S' shape.

Citrus loops. Halve fruit through stem end; slice cross-wise. Separate all but 1 inch of peel from fruit. Curl under.

Fringed citrus. Halve orange or grapefruit. With sharp knife, cut slashes at angle around top edge of peel.

How to Make Cucumber Twists

Frosted grapes. Cut small clusters of grapes. Dip in lightly beaten egg white, then granulated or colored sugar. Set on rack to dry.

Divide unpeeled cucumber in 2-in. lengths. Cut ¼-in. thick slices off sides: trim slices to ½ inch wide.

Make 2 lengthwise cuts, one on each end, leaving ½ inch attached at the end of each cut in each strip. Twist the outer strips so they cross.

How to Make Citrus Fruit Baskets

Halve grapefruit or large orange. Hollow out shell. Combine citrus sections with other fresh or canned fruits.

Cut ¼-in. wide strip around edge of fruit shell, leaving 1 inch of peel attached on each side.

Fill shells with mixed fruits. Pull strips together at the top and fasten with picks. Decorate with mint leaves.

Simple Dinner for Four

A simple dinner becomes a party when well-cooked food is served with flair. In this menu, the food, rather than the setting, provides the decorative element.

Present the tomato-garnished fish and rice on a plain serving plate trimmed with sprigs of parsley to echo the color of broccoli. A simple cut and twist transforms lemon slices into a decorative vegetable garnish.

Set off the colorful salad with a glass or wooden bowl. You could serve the rice in a one-of-a-kind bowl from an old set of dishes.

A low-key setting provides a background for the food. For a centerpiece, set a flourishing house plant in a basket, or cluster several small plants, using extra table napkins and contrasting ribbon to cover the pots.

Menu

Orange-Endive Salad
Garnished with red onion rings, page 131

Saffron Brown Rice
page 123

Wine-Poached Fish
Delicately seasoned fillets with sliced tomato, page 105

Lemony Broccoli
page 111

Mocha Pudding
Cool and creamy blend of chocolate and coffee, page 149

Time Management

The night before or early in the day, microwave pudding, pour into dishes, place plastic wrap directly on pudding and chill. Section oranges; wrap and refrigerate. Remaining salad ingredients can be prepared early in the day or while rice is cooking.

About 1 hour before serving time, microwave rice. Assemble and refrigerate salad. Prepare broccoli and fish to cook. While rice stands, partially cook broccoli 5 minutes at High. Set aside while microwaving fish.

While fish stands, microwave broccoli 4 to 8 minutes. Set aside while you prepare sauce and slice lemon for garnish.

Reheat rice at High 1 to 3 minutes. Complete broccoli and decorate with lemon twists. Remove fish to serving plate and garnish with parsley. Toss salad with dressing just before serving or pass the dressing separately in a cruet or sauce bowl.

Dinner Party for Eight

This menu deserves your best china, flatware and linen. Choose a low, elegant floral arrangement. Pictured is a white-on-white setting, accented with floating carnations. Behind each place setting, on the left side, arrange a small candle set in a glass, so each guest is provided with a light.

The focal points for this very special dinner party are a dramatic crown roast of pork and the Black Forest cake. Order the meat several days in advance and have the butcher tie the pork loin in a circle and remove the backbone. Pick roast up the day of the party.

The advance preparation can be done the day before or early the day of the party. For greater leisure, spread preparation over two days.

Final preparation time depends on the weight of your roast and how quickly your oven cooks food. Assemble the dessert just before you start the roast.

The most accurate way to microwave a crown roast is by temperature. The times given are an approximate guide so you will know about how long cooking will take.

Insert a microwave thermometer or automatic temperature probe between two of the ribs in the roast. The point should rest in the meaty area inside the crown, without touching fat or bone. The roast should stand 10 minutes after microwaving, and will hold for an additional 20 minutes, giving you plenty of time to microwave the vegetable, decorate the roast and place the food on the table.

Menu

Relish Tray
Assorted pickles and raw vegetables

Spiced Apple Relish
A sweet and savory complement to roast pork, page 126

Crown Roast of Pork
Stuffed with fruited meat dressing, page 96

Peas & Artichokes
Classic combination from Italy, page 114

Black Forest Cake
An inspired confection of chocolate, cherries and whipped cream, page 142

Time Management

Day before or early in the day, prepare and refrigerate apple relish.

Microwave cake and cherry filling; refrigerate. Chill bowl and beaters for whipped cream. Microwave and refrigerate stuffing for roast.

Cut up raw vegetables for relish tray. Place in bowl of ice water and refrigerate to crisp.

Estimate roasting time for pork, so you will know when to begin completing the meal.

About 20 mintues before starting roast, remove apple relish, stuffing and cherry filling from refrigerator. Whip cream; refrigerate while slicing cake. Assemble cake and chill until serving time.

About 2 to 2½ hours before serving time, start pork roast. While pork is cooking, drain relish vegetables. Arrange on tray with pickles and olives. Cover and refrigerate.

Thirty minutes before roast is done, fill center with stuffing. Cover stuffing with plastic wrap. Microwave until internal temperature of roast reaches 165°F., checking several places.

Let roast stand, tented with foil. Microwave peas and artichokes. When temperature of roast reaches 170°F., remove to serving plate, using spatula to support stuffing. Decorate roast with paper frills and spiced peaches; cover loosely with foil. Microwave vegetables.

Cocktail Party
Buffet for Eight

When you give a cocktail party, some guests will visit briefly on their way to dinner, others may arrive later in the evening, while some may stay for the entire party.

The food for this buffet can be eaten with your fingers or cocktail picks from small plates as your guests move about the room conversing. Guests can eat lightly, while those who do not go on to dinner can eat a balanced menu of protein, bread and vegetables.

This party was planned for eight people. If you wish to serve more guests, don't double the recipes. Instead, add other dishes from the appetizer section of this book. Look for recipes which can be prepared in advance or served cold, and try to maintain the balance of meats, cheese or fish, bread stuffs and vegetables.

Cover your table with heavy-duty foil, shiny side up. Place white candles of various heights in every candle holder you own, and line them up in the center of the table. If you don't have enough different candle holders to make an effective display, use florists' clay to hold the tapers in wine and water goblets. Arrange greens on the table between the candles.

Menu

Party Quiche
Cheese, bacon and custard in a flaky crust, page 107

Sirloin Teriyaki
Marinated steak strips, page 91

Spinach-Filled Bread
Colorful spread in a bread case, page 85

Vegetables Provençal
Marinated cauliflower, carrots, peppers and black olives, page 119

Time Management

One or 2 days before the party, prepare vegetables. Cover; marinate in the refrigerator.

The day before, marinate steak strips. Prepare quiche and refrigerate, covered with plastic wrap.

Early in the day, hollow out bread case; wrap in foil or plastic. Cut bread in cubes; place in plastic bag to keep fresh. Microwave bacon; drain.

Defrost spinach; combine with remaining ingredients for filling. Refrigerate.

Half an hour before serving time, microwave steak strips. Cover dish with foil; it will stay warm 30 to 40 minutes.

Microwave spinach mixture at High 30 seconds to 1¼ minutes while you cut quiche. Place pieces on oven-safe platter and cover with wax paper. Reheat quiche at 50% (Medium) 3 to 6 minutes, rearranging pieces once. Fill bread case with spinach mixture and arrange cubed bread around it.

Spring Open House
Buffet for Twenty

Because of the advance preparation, this party leaves little work to be done at the last minute. Try it for a shower or following a graduation. The chicken or turkey can be microwaved the day before the party, or you can substitute a 3-lb. piece of cooked boneless turkey breast from the deli section of your market.

The buffet can be served in either a single or double line. If you want the guests to form two lines, arrange each food in two serving dishes, one for each side of the table.

To cover the table, buy a wallpaper remnant in a floral pattern. Cut three pieces, each the table length plus 2 feet for a drop at both ends. If you wish, scallop the ends of the paper, using a plate as a guide.

In the center of the table, lay flowering branches from the garden, or arrange a row of small bouquets or pots of spring flowers. If you set up a separate table for the punch bowl, decorate that with wallpaper and branches, too.

Menu

Fruit Punch in Watermelon Bowl
Served in sugar-frosted glasses garnished with whole strawberries, page 88

Fruit With Raspberry Dip
Assorted fresh fruits with a colorful sour cream dip, page 125

Hot Chicken Salad
Brandied chicken with grapes, almonds and shredded lettuce, page 105

Spiced Nuts
Savory buttered nuts, page 83

Assorted Bakery Rolls

Petits Fours
Tiny glazed cakes, page 145

Time Management

Several days in advance, prepare nuts. When dry, store in tightly covered container.

The day before the party, cook and cube chicken or turkey. Cover and refrigerate. Microwave cake layers. After cooling, wrap in plastic or foil. Microwave syrup for punch. Set aside to cool.

No more than 24 hours before serving time, make melon balls and watermelon punch bowl. Refrigerate. Frost, decorate and chill punch glasses.

Early in the day, microwave frosting for petit fours. While frosting cools to 110°F., prepare salad ingredients. Combine all except lettuce and grapes. Cover and refrigerate. Frost and decorate petit fours. Add berries and fruit juices to punch syrup; chill.

Prepare all fruits except banana chunks. To prevent discoloration, dip apple and pear wedges in lemon juice. Cover and refrigerate.

When guests arrive, add carbonated water and ice to punch. Pour into watermelon bowl and serve in frosted glasses.

Fifteen to 20 minutes before serving, microwave chicken mixture 10 to 15 minutes at High, or until heated, stirring once or twice.

While chicken is heating, cut up banana pieces for fruit dip. Toss with lemon juice. Combine ingredients for raspberry dip. Arrange fruits on a bed of ice with bowl of dip in center.

Add lettuce and grapes to heated chicken salad and serve.

After the Game
Buffet for Ten to Twelve

After an outdoor event, serve this colorful and satisfying meal. Advance preparation allows you to attend the game, then bring your guests home. As soon as you arrive, serve a hot dip to take the edge off fresh air appetites while you reheat the chili.

The full recipe of chili reheats in 45 minutes to

Menu

Jalapeño Cheese Dip
Blend of cheeses with a touch of hot pepper, page 80

Texas Chili
Classic chili with chunks of beef, page 92

Shredded Lettuce Salad
Layered salad with spicy
sour cream dressing, page 129

Mexican Sundaes
Cinnamon-fudge sauce over ice cream, page 149

an hour. If you wish to serve supper sooner than that, heat the chili in two batches. Your guests can start on the first while the second is heating.

Cafeteria-style service fits the casual atmosphere of this party. For each guest, provide a tray lined with a page from the sports section of the newspaper. Next to the stacked

trays, arrange plates, napkins and flatware in mugs or pots.

As a centerpiece, use knit caps in team colors to cover the pots of chrysanthemum plants, or cut a hole in a toy football and use it as a container for fall flowers or pompons.

Time Management

The day before the party, microwave chili. After standing, cover and refrigerate.

When you and guests return from the game, microwave Jalapeño Cheese Dip and serve.

Divide chili into two 2-qt. covered casseroles. Microwave one at a time at 70% (Medium-High) 15 to 20 minutes, or until heated, stirring once or twice. While chili is heating,

combine ingredients for salad and dressing. Interrupt the heating of the second batch of chili to warm the salad dressing. Let guests start with the first casserole of chili and the salad. Serve the second batch of chili when it is ready.

After the meal, combine ingredients for cinnamon-fudge sauce. Microwave while scooping ice cream.

Adult Birthday Party
Dinner for Eight

A grown-up birthday party calls for a menu in the light, contemporary style. This one is varied to please the eye and deftly seasoned for adult tastes. Like any true birthday party, it includes cake and ice cream, which are presented in a grown-up version.

A formal table setting would be appropriate for the menu, but for this occasion, contrast the adult food with a whimsical setting, reminiscent of childhood parties. Cover the table with white shelf paper or brown wrapping paper. As a favor for each guest, provide a box of crayons.

Menu

Wineberry Salad
Creamy cranberry and sangria gelatin, page 134

Sweet & Sour Green Beans
Beans in piquant sauce with bacon
and onion rings, page 110

Chicken With Sherried Cheese Sauce
Crumb-crisped chicken breasts with
Swiss cheese sauce, page 101

Wild Rice Medley
Festive combination of wild rice
and mushrooms, page 122

Ice Cream-Filled Cake
Sophisticated version of birthday cake
and ice cream, page 146

Time Management

The day before the party, prepare cake; fill and freeze.

Early in the day, make gelatin; chill. Cut up bacon and onion for beans. Refrigerate in plastic bag. Chop onion and celery for rice. Combine and refrigerate, covered. Wash and slice mushrooms. Cover and refrigerate.

About 1¼ to 1½ hours before serving time, microwave bacon and onion rings while you wash wild rice. Add remaining sauce ingredients to bacon mixture; set aside.

Melt butter for chicken and combine rice with hot water. While rice is cooking, coat chicken with crumbs and arrange on microwave baking sheet. When rice is tender, set aside, covered, to keep warm. Microwave chicken until no longer pink. Let stand, covered.

Unmold salad and return to refrigerator while you microwave green beans. Set beans aside, covered. Microwave onion, celery and mushrooms for rice.

Prepare sauce for chicken while you drain rice and combine with vegetables. Add beans to bacon mixture. Heat rice at High 3 to 4 minutes, and beans 2 to 3 minutes while you sauce and garnish chicken breasts.

After the meal, microwave chocolate sauce for cake while clearing the table.

Midnight Supper for Six

After the theater or a dance, bring your friends home to a light, continental supper. Since the preparation is done early in the day, the meal can be ready to serve within half an hour of the time you arrive home. Heat the shrimp appetizer in 3 to 4 minutes. While your guests enjoy their appetizer, put finishing touches to the meal.

The theme for this setting is the midnight sky. For a royal or navy blue tablecloth, use a sheet or inexpensive remnant. Place a wine cooler in the center of the table with wine glasses around it. Fold napkins in a fan shape and tuck them into the glasses. On the dark blue cloth, scatter silver stars from a stationer's or variety store.

Menu

Shrimp Wrap-Ups
Bacon-wrapped shrimp and green pepper
in plum sauce, page 79

Double Cheese Quiche
Light, crustless quiche, page 106

Garlic Bread
page 137

Fruit Kabobs
Honey-glazed fresh fruits, page 125

White Wine

Time Management

Early in the day, prepare Shrimp Wrap-Ups. Add sauce and refrigerate. Microwave quiche. Cover and refrigerate. Prepare fruit kabobs, taking care to glaze thoroughly so apple and banana chunks will not discolor. Prepare garlic bread.

When you and the guests arrive, preheat conventional oven and start garlic bread.

Microwave Shrimp Wrap-Ups at High 3 to 4 minutes. Serve as appetizer. Reheat quiche at 50% (Medium) 10 to 15 minutes, rotating ½ turn once or twice. While quiche is heating, place ice and wine in cooler and glaze fruit.

From the Freezer:
Impromptu Dinner for Two

This dinner can be ready in less than an hour. The appetizer and vegetables are made quickly from frozen foods. The main dish and rice are made in advance, frozen and easily defrosted when you feel like inviting a guest for dinner, even at the last minute.

The dessert makes it a party...not just a piece of chocolate cake but a whole miniature cake made for two. It's in the freezer ready for a special occasion. If you don't have time to finish the cake before your guest arrives, it can be defrosted while you are eating dinner and frosted just before serving.

Serve this impromptu party in an unusual place: a coffee table in front of the fire, a card table set by a window, or picnic table on a deck.

Menu

Polynesian Appetizers
Glazed nuggets of pineapple and sausage, page 79

Pepper Steak
page 92

Long Grain Rice
page 122

Sunny Carrots
page 112

Chocolate Cake
Just the right size for two, page 141

Time Management

Before your guest arrives, unwrap cake layers and place on paper towel-lined plate. Microwave at 50% (Medium) 2 to 6 minutes, or until wooden pick inserted in center meets little resistance, rearranging once. Let stand. Frost cake and assemble appetizer.

When guest arrives, microwave appetizer at High 3 to 7 minutes, stirring 2 or 3 times. Serve.

About 30 to 45 minutes before serving time, place rice in 1-qt. casserole; cover. Microwave at High 5 to 10 minutes, or until hot, stirring once or twice. Let stand, covered. Place Pepper Steak in 1-qt. casserole; cover. Microwave; add cornstarch as directed in recipe. Set aside, covered. Microwave carrots.

From the Freezer:
Dinner for Two

A spur-of-the-moment party is not the only time when the freezer and microwave oven team up to simplify entertaining. When some of the dishes are prepared and frozen in advance, you can plan a party for a busy day and still have time to serve a very special meal.

For this menu, the raw chicken breasts are stuffed and frozen. They keep up to a month and are microwaved from the frozen state in about 20 minutes.

The individual cheesecakes can be prepared

and frozen up to 2 weeks ahead. They are frozen, defrosted and served in the same custard cups.

Depending on your schedule, the versatile salad can be prepared at any time from the evening before up to the last minute. It tastes equally good warm or chilled.

A table for two is an occasion to try the unexpected. Instead of sitting face-to-face, sit on adjoining sides of the table and use the opposite corner for food.

Menu

Chicken Roulades
Stuffed chicken breasts with mushroom sauce, page 103

Citrus Salad
Honey-glazed orange and grapefruit sections, page 130

Asparagus Spears
Garnished with sunflower nuts, page 109

Almond Cheesecake
Individual cheesecakes, page 147

Time Management

Night before or early in the day, you can section oranges and grapefruit. Microwave dressing; toss with fruit. Cover and refrigerate.

About 1 hour before serving time, microwave frozen chicken breasts at High 5 minutes. Reduce power to 50% (Medium). Microwave 9 to 14 minutes, or until meat is no longer pink, rearranging after half the time.

Set chicken aside while microwaving asparagus and preparing ingredients for

mushroom sauce.

Let asparagus stand, covered, while microwaving mushroom sauce. Add melted butter and wine to asparagus; top with sunflower nuts.

After the meal, unwrap cheesecakes. Microwave at 50% (Medium) 1 to 3 minutes, or until wooden pick inserted in center meets little resistance, checking frequently. Serve in the custard cups.

From the Freezer:
Cocktail Party for Ten to Twelve

A cocktail party is one of the easiest ways to entertain, especially when you have a microwave oven. Prepare the food in your spare time, and store it in the freezer.

At a cocktail party, all the food does not have to be hot and ready to eat at the same time. To get things started, microwave a few items and serve them as they are ready. This gives you plenty of time to talk to your guests, cook the shrimp, and reheat the chicken.

Foods for a cocktail party can be served in any way which is convenient for you. You may ask some of your guests to pass the plates; this can be a good ice-breaker when the guests are not already acquainted. To encourage guests to circulate, you can set out the food in several places: a coffee table, end tables, even a desk. If you want the guests to congregate, choose a dining table as a serving area. However you decide to serve the food, provide plenty of small paper plates, napkins and cocktail picks.

Menu

Marinated Brussels Sprouts
Cocktail Brussels sprouts in a tangy marinade, page 112

Shrimp in Beer
Tiny shrimp served hot, page 78

Crab Canapés
Hot crab meat mixture on melba rounds, page 84

Miniature Chicken Drumsticks
Sesame-coated chicken wings, page 81

Ham Salad Finger Rolls
Ham salad rolled in whole wheat bread, page 83

Sausage Balls
Pork sausage-flavored with Parmesan cheese, page 83

Spinach Balls
Spinach combined with Swiss and Parmesan cheese, page 83

Time Management

During the 2 weeks preceding the party, prepare the sausage and spinach balls, chicken drumsticks, crab canapés and ham finger rolls at your convenience. You'll have time to make a dish in the evening, freeze it overnight, and package for freezer storage the next day. You may want to make 2 or 3 batches of the ham salad finger rolls; they go fast during a party.

The night before the party, microwave the Brussels sprouts. Cover and marinate in the refrigerator overnight.

Half an hour before the party, set out Brussels sprouts.

When guests arrive, place 24 sausage balls on a 12-in. paper towel-lined plate. Microwave at High 1½ to 3½ minutes, or until firm to touch and heated, rearranging once. Serve.

While sausage balls are heating, assemble 18 crab canapés on a 12-in. paper towel-lined plate. Microwave at 70% (Medium-High) 1¾ to 3 minutes, or until heated, rearranging after half the time. Serve.

Place spinach balls on paper towel-lined baking sheet. Microwave at High 2 minutes. Reduce power to 50% (Medium). Microwave 4½ to 6 minutes, or until hot and just set, rearranging spinach balls once or twice. Transfer to platter and serve. While heating spinach balls, arrange 36 slices of ham finger rolls around the edge of a 12-in. plate. Microwave at High 3 to 6 minutes, or until hot, rotating plate once or twice. Serve.

While guests enjoy these appetizers, microwave and serve shrimp and reheat chicken wings 11 to 15 minutes at High, rotating baking sheet 2 or 3 times.

Microwave additional plates of sausage balls, crab canapés and finger rolls as needed.

From the Freezer:
Dinner for Two to Twelve

Spaghetti sauce is an excellent choice when you want to stock your freezer with the makings of a party. It's as easy to microwave in quantity as it is in small batches.

This recipe makes enough sauce for 12 people. Freeze it in two-serving portions, and you'll be ready for an impromptu supper for 12 or several smaller parties. In addition to flexibility in the size of your party, small batch freezing has two other advantages: small packages freeze rapidly and during defrosting there is less need to stir or break up frozen portions, which leaves you more time to attend to the rest of the meal.

Whether the party is a spur-of-the-moment invitation or planned in advance, this menu is a good choice for after a game or the theater.

For an authentic touch, serve the spaghetti on soup plates or dinner plates with a deep rim, which are similar to Italian pasta plates. Italians eat spaghetti by pulling out a few strands with a fork, then turning the tines of the fork against the side of the pasta plate until the spaghetti is rolled around the fork. In America, the fork can be used with a soup spoon.

Menu

Italian Spaghetti
Ground beef and Italian sausage in tomato sauce, page 95

Tossed Salad
page 129

Bakery Breads

Chocolate Amaretto Sundae
Almond-flavored sauce served over spumoni ice cream, page 149

Time Management

Up to a week in advance, the chocolate Amaretto sauce can be microwaved and refrigerated. If the party is an impromptu affair, microwave sauce after dinner.

About 15 to 45 minutes before serving, remove enough two-serving packages of spaghetti sauce from the freezer to serve the number of guests.

Place frozen sauce in casserole; cover. If lid does not fit at first, microwave at High for first 5 minutes, then break up sauce with fork and cover. Microwave at High, stirring 2 or 3 times during cooking. Time will depend on number of servings used.

While sauce is heating, cook spaghetti conventionally and combine salad ingredients in bowl. If chocolate Amaretto sauce has not been prepared in advance, measure and mix the ingredients.

After the meal, microwave or reheat dessert sauce while scooping spumoni ice cream.

From the Freezer:
Buffet for Ten to Twelve

This menu features cold sliced turkey and hot roast beef with gravy. In the assortment of rolls, include some split hard rolls and small buns, so guests can make sandwiches if they like. Decorative potato rosettes are made in advance and reheated straight from the freezer. The frozen turkey breast is defrosted and cooked the day before, while the sirloin tip is microwaved from the frozen state without preliminary defrosting.

At most buffets, breads follow the main dishes and salad, so guests can place a roll on their plates just before they pick up their silverware. With this menu, some guests may want to make sandwiches, so the breads should be arranged next to the meat platters. Allow space for the guests to put down their plates while they assemble a sandwich. Serve the beverage from a separate table, if necessary.

After the meal, clear the table and reset it to serve the dessert, or pass the dessert to your guests with fresh forks and napkins.

Menu

Sirloin Tip Roast
page 92

Turkey Breast
page 102

Assorted Bakery Rolls

Potato Rosettes
Fluffy mashed potato stars, page 116

Vegetables Mornay
Medley of vegetables in cheese sauce, page 119

Pound Cake & Strawberries
page 145

Time Management

A week before the party, prepare and freeze Potato Rosettes.

The day before, defrost and microwave turkey breast. Cool, then slice thinly. Arrange slices on microwave oven-safe platter. Cover with plastic wrap and refrigerate.

Early in the day, rinse, hull and halve strawberries. Sprinkle with sugar. Refrigerate, covered. Chill bowl and beaters for cream. Split sandwich rolls. Arrange breads in basket. Cover with plastic wrap.

About 1¾ to 2 hours before serving time, start frozen sirloin tip roast. While roast is cooking, slice carrots and measure ingredients for Vegetables Mornay.

While roast stands, microwave vegetables and mix ingredients for gravy.

Drain vegetables, add mushrooms and set aside, covered. Microwave covered platter of sliced turkey at High 1 to 3 minutes to remove chill.

Microwave gravy and set aside, covered. Prepare mornay sauce and croutons. While carving the roast, reheat vegetables at High 2 to 4 minutes. Gently stir in sauce. Microwave at High 4 to 5 minutes, adding croutons during the last minute of cooking time.

Arrange 15 potato rosettes on a 12-in. plate. Cover with wax paper. While you place food on buffet table, microwave Potato Rosettes at 70% (Medium-High) 7 to 11 minutes, rearranging after 5 minutes. Reheat gravy at High 1 to 4 minutes, if needed.

While guests serve themselves, microwave remaining rosettes as needed.

After the meal, defrost and slice pound cakes; whip cream. Top cake slices with strawberries and whipped cream.

Foreign Affair: Oriental Dinner for Six to Eight

To Western eyes, a Chinese meal for more than two people looks like a feast. The number of main dishes served increases with the number of guests. At this meal there are four main dishes. All are served at the same time and guests sample each one.

If cooked conventionally, the menu would keep the cook watching and stirring four pots at once. With a microwave oven, you cook the dishes one at a time and reheat briefly, if needed.

To simplify Oriental cooking, get all the ingredients ready in advance. The actual microwaving time will depend on the speed of your oven. If your oven cooks food very fast, cooking will take about an hour and only the pork should need reheating. With a slower cooking oven, cooking and reheating will take under 2 hours.

Set the table with a white or lacquer-red cloth. At a Chinese meal, the food provides the centerpiece. To keep main dishes hot, serve from the casseroles they were microwaved in.

You don't need special Oriental dishes, but by all means, use them if you have them. At each place, set a dinner plate with a bowl or mug centered on it. In China, guests drink the soup, then set the bowl aside to hold rice, which is never eaten from the same plate as other main dishes. Bamboo chopsticks add to the Oriental atmosphere, but provide forks for guests who prefer them. To conclude the meal, pass a basket of refreshing hot finger towels (oshibori).

Menu

Egg Drop Soup
Clear soup with beaten eggs, page 87

Steamed Vegetables
Soy-glazed vegetables, page 119

Chicken & Pea Pods
Traditional combination with a hint of fresh ginger, page 104

Red-Glazed Pork
Tenderloin with vegetables, page 98

Shrimp & Rice
page 123

Floating Almond Dessert
Almond-flavored milk gelatin, page 148

Time Management

Several days in advance, prepare gelatin and sauce for the dessert. Cover and refrigerate separately until just before serving.

The night before, slice meats and vegetables for each recipe. Cover; refrigerate.

Early in the day, combine cornstarch and sauce mixtures in small bowls. Set aside. Chop green onion for rice and soup.

Prepare eight oshibori towels. Moisten well. Place in a basket and cover to keep damp.

About 1 to 2 hours before serving time, microwave rice. Set aside, covered. Prepare soup. It will keep warm, covered, for 30 to 35 minutes.

Microwave Red-Glazed Pork, Chicken & Pea Pods and Steamed Vegetables. After microwaving each dish, cover and set aside.

If necessary, reheat soup at High 1 to 2 minutes. Pour into mugs or drinking bowls, sprinkle with green onions and serve.

While guests drink the soup, reheat pork at High 2 to 5 minutes. If necessary, reheat chicken 1 to 2 minutes and rice 2 to 3 minutes. Serve all the main dishes at the same time.

After the meal, assemble Floating Almond Dessert and serve.

After the dessert, microwave the basket of towels 30 to 60 seconds, or until hot. Pass to guests so they can wipe their fingers.

Foreign Affair: Italian

Dinner for Eight

The food for this party is prepared in advance. At serving time, all you do is heat the main dish.

Before Italian cooks had home ovens, they carried manicotti to the village oven for baking. Now, when pasta is baked at home, they still let it "settle" 10 to 20 minutes, the time it took to bring the food home.

Except for the green pepper strips, the

Menu

Antipasto
Before the pasta, a tray of cheese, meat and pickled vegetables, page 132

Giardiniera Salad
Vegetables marinated in fragrant olive oil and vinegar dressing, page 132

Manicotti
Stuffed pasta tubes topped with tomato sauce and cheese, page 94

Bakery Bread

Cappuccino
Served with an assortment of cookies from the gourmet section of your store or with fruit and cheese, page 89

antipasto is assembled with foods that require no preparation. Arrange the items in a decorative pattern to suit the shape of your tray.

The colors of the Italian flag inspire this table setting. Use a plain white cloth. Make a red and a green runner, each one-third as wide as the table. Place one on each side under the plates.

As a centerpiece, use a candelabra or group several pillar candles of varying heights. On each dinner plate, set a smaller plate for the antipasto course. Place the bread sticks in a glass, or lay a crusty loaf directly on the table cloth. Guests break off pieces, Italian style.

Time Management

The day before, microwave the salad. Cover and refrigerate. The salad could be prepared on the morning of the party, but will taste even better if allowed to marinate overnight.

Early in the day, drain olives, artichoke hearts, pickled peppers and anchovies. Slice cheese and green pepper; roll up meats. Arrange antipasto on serving tray. Cover; refrigerate. Prepare cookie plate or fruit bowl.

Prepare manicotti shells and filling; assemble. Cover and refrigerate. Prepare sauce. Cover and refrigerate.

About 45 minutes before serving, remove manicotti and sauce from refrigerator. Microwave sauce at High 2 to 3 minutes, or until hot. Pour sauce over shells. Microwave each dish at High 8 minutes while preparing topping. Spoon half of topping on first dish. Microwave at 70% (Medium-High) 7 to 10 minutes, rotating once or twice. Repeat with second dish.

After dinner, microwave cappuccino. Serve with cookies or fruit and cheese.

Foreign Affair: East Indian

Dinner for Six to Eight

The name, Five Boy Curry, refers to the number of servants needed to present the small dishes of condiments which are traditional with curries. At a Western dinner party, the condiments help decorate the table as well as garnish the food. Brass, mirrors and brilliant colors create an Indian atmosphere.

For a tablecloth, use an Indian cotton, such as a woven bedspread, a colorful print or a Madras plaid. Repeat one of the colors with cloth or paper napkins. For a centerpiece, cluster an assortment of brass candlesticks, or float a few large flowers in a brass bowl.

This menu is designed so that most of the preparation can be done well in advance, leaving the day of the party free until just before the guests arrive. The chicken could be cooked just before serving, but tastes even better when flavors have a chance to mellow. While it reheats, you will have time to spend with your guests.

Menu

Lamb Meatballs
Appetizers in spicy sauce, page 99

Marinated Vegetable Salad
Tomatoes, cucumbers and onion in minted lemon juice and olive oil, page 134

Riz Indienne
Fluffy pilaf with raisins, page 123

Five Boy Chicken Curry
Served with small bowls of almonds, toasted coconut, crumbled crisp bacon, watermelon pickles, chopped hard cooked egg, page 103

Fresh Fruit Chutney
Sweet and tangy fruit relish, page 126

Honey Cake
Honey glazed citrus and spice cake, page 143

Darjeeling Tea

Time Management

Two to 3 weeks in advance, microwave honey cake. Remove from pan, but do not glaze. Cool, wrap, label and freeze.

One week in advance, prepare fruit chutney. Cover and refrigerate.

The day before, assemble and refrigerate marinated vegetables. Microwave meatballs. Drain, cover and refrigerate but do not prepare sauce. Prepare Chicken Curry, but do not add cream. Cover and refrigerate.

Early in the day, measure all ingredients except hot water for meatball sauce and Riz Indienne. Combine glaze ingredients. Place condiments in small bowls. Set aside until ready to use.

When guests arrive, prepare sauce. Stir in meatballs; cover. Microwave at High 3 to 7 minutes, or until hot, stirring once or twice. Serve as an appetizer.

About an hour before serving time, remove chicken from refrigerator. Microwave rice. Set aside, tightly covered, to complete cooking and keep warm. To reheat chicken, uncover and microwave at High 20 to 28 minutes, or until hot. Arrange chicken on platter. Stir cream into sauce.

After the dinner, unwrap frozen honey cake. Place on serving plate and pierce with fork. Microwave at 50% (Medium) 2 to 4 minutes, or until defrosted and warm. Heat glaze and pour over cake as directed.

Foreign Affair: Spanish

Dinner for Six to Eight

A party for six to eight can be as easy to serve as dinner for two. This festive meal takes less than an hour of microwaving time. Allow another hour for leisurely preparation. If you have the

---

Menu

Mediterranean Salad
Lettuce, asparagus, anchovies with
oil and vinegar, page 133

Saffron Rice
Long grain rice seasoned with garlic
and saffron, page 123

Spanish Chicken
Tender chicken breasts in wine sauce, page 102

Braised Green Peppers
Green pepper and onion in garlic and olive oil, page 115

Poached Oranges
Orange sections in sangria, page 127

time, prepare the ingredients early in the day.

Color and texture in food and setting carry out the Spanish theme. Straw mats or a plain tablecloth provide a background for patterned pottery. Wrap the stem of a bright paper flower around each rolled napkin. A mixture of patterns reflects the Moorish influence in southern Spain.

Time Management

Early in the day, prepare and microwave oranges; refrigerate.

Cut peppers into strips. Slice and separate onion rings. Refrigerate in plastic bag.

Layer olives, mushrooms and chicken. Microwave and drain the bacon.

About 45 minutes to an hour before serving time, prepare and microwave sauce. Pour over chicken and microwave.

While chicken is cooking, measure ingredients for rice and assemble pepper casserole. Set chicken aside. Microwave rice, then peppers. Arrange salads on plates. If necessary, reheat chicken 2 to 5 minutes at High before serving.

New Year's Eve
Buffet for Six to Eight

Your New Year's Eve party might be a dinner served to friends who gather at your house before going on to a theater or dance, or it could be an at-home affair, with the food served as a late evening supper.

This flexible menu may be presented in several ways to suit your plans. For an early evening party, you can omit one of the appetizers and serve the cake right after dinner. The fruit salad is sweet enough to double as a dessert with the meal, so if guests stay through the evening, offer the cake with coffee after midnight.

Serve the food from a table or kitchen counter if you don't have a buffet. Arrange dinner plates at one end of the buffet, and napkins and flatware at the other. Set out mats or trivets for the serving dishes and scatter paper streamers and confetti around them.

Menu

Curry Dip
Fresh vegetable dippers with creamy curry dip, page 81

Spiced Shrimp
Shrimp in spicy white sauce, page 78

Chicken & Rice
Chicken, peanuts and rice casserole, page 105

Broccoli & Mushrooms
Marinated in Italian dressing, page 111

Lemon-Ginger Fruit Salad
Fresh fruits in lemon-ginger dressing, page 130

Lemon Ring Cake
page 144

Time Management

The day before, microwave chicken. Cover and refrigerate skinned chicken and reserved broth. Prepare the fruit salad, omitting cherries. Cover and refrigerate. Prepare and marinate broccoli and mushrooms.

Early in the day, microwave and frost ring cake. Prepare curry dip and vegetables. Chop onion for rice. Cover and refrigerate. Peel and devein shrimp. Cover; refrigerate.

When guests arrive, soften curry dip. Microwave shrimp and serve as an appetizer.

About 35 to 40 minutes before serving time, remove chicken from refrigerator. Heat broth at High 2 to 4 minutes. Microwave rice. Set aside, covered. Microwave chicken at High 1 to 4 minutes, or until heated. Add to rice with peanuts. Let stand, covered, while you place broccoli and mushrooms in serving dish. Add cherries to fruit salad, if desired.

After dinner, or at the end of the party, serve cake with coffee.

New Year's Day
Buffet for Twenty

With a well-planned menu, the microwave oven can cook food for a crowd as smoothly as for an intimate party. Most of the cooking for this buffet is done in advance. The ham is microwaved just long enough to remove the chill, which makes it easy to carve and eliminates the problem of keeping it hot. Because the melba crackers are very crisp, the canapés can be assembled a few hours before the party, or while you are microwaving the hot foods, whichever is more convenient.

With 20 guests, it's important to plan for a smooth flow of traffic. If possible, arrange the buffet in an open area or a room with two entrances, so guests with full plates won't cross paths with people waiting in line.

Next to each serving dish, allow space where guests can set their plates down as they serve themselves. The silverware, napkins and beverage are placed at the end of the buffet so guests won't have their hands full as they move through the line. If your table is small, the beverage can be set on another table, out of the way of the buffet. The dessert for this menu may be placed on the table with the rest of the meal, or passed to guests later.

Menu

Florentine Canapés
Parmesan spinach spread mounded on melba rounds, page 84

Black-Eyed Peas
A Southern tradition on New Year's Day, page 114

Glazed Ham
Mustard and brown sugar add gloss and flavor, page 98

Lemon-Buttered Brussels Sprouts
Miniature cabbages in tangy butter sauce, page 111

Assorted Bakery Rolls

Apricot Chews
Tart and rich cookies with powdered sugar, page 152

Time Management

Up to 2 days before the party, prepare and refrigerate Apricot Chews.

The day before, microwave black-eyed peas and spinach spread. Glaze ham; microwave to set glaze. Refrigerate all, covered.

About 2 to 3 hours before serving time, assemble canapés. Arrange on paper towel-lined plates. Cover; refrigerate. If more convenient, prepare canapés later, while microwaving the peas and Brussels sprouts.

About 1 to 1¼ hours before serving time, microwave peas at High 20 to 30 minutes, or until hot, stirring 2 or 3 times. Let stand, covered. They will keep warm up to 1 hour.

Start Brussels sprouts. While heating peas and cooking Brussels sprouts, arrange Apricot Chews on serving plate and return to the refrigerator. Set out the rolls. Assemble canapés if you have not done so already.

When sprouts are tender, set aside, covered. Microwave ham at High 5 to 10 minutes, or until glaze is reheated. Prepare lemon sauce for Brussels sprouts.

While you carve the ham and finish the Brussels sprouts, ask a guest to microwave a plate or two of canapés. The remaining canapés can be heated as needed, after the guests have started the buffet.

Valentine's Day
Dinner for Two

For this romantic dinner advance preparation will simplify the minutes before your guest arrives. The veal also develops additional flavor.

If you have an old piece of crocheted or tatted lace, place it over a red or pink cloth to carry out the valentine theme. To create this lacy effect in a contemporary style, arrange white paper doilies over the cloth. A single rose and a pair of candles complete the setting.

Menu

Lettuce Cups
Iceberg lettuce with hot bacon dressing, page 129

Broccoli Spears
page 120

Creamy Veal
Tender veal served over fettuccine, page 98

Cappuccino for Two
Dessert coffee, page 89

Grapes & Cheese

Time Management

The day before, cook veal. Cover; refrigerate.

Early in the day, prepare lettuce, tomato and egg for salad, but do not assemble. Cover and refrigerate. Wash and drain grapes; arrange in fruit bowl. Cover and refrigerate. Trim unwashed broccoli. Cover and refrigerate.

About 20 to 25 minutes before serving time, cook fettuccine conventionally. Microwave and drain bacon. Prepare salad dressing and set aside.

Rinse broccoli and microwave. Let stand, covered. Reheat veal at 50% (Medium) 4 to 9 minutes while arranging salads on plate.

Pour veal over drained noodles while heating dressing 30 to 45 seconds. Spoon dressing over salads.

After the meal, serve a light dessert of grapes with cheese. As a finale, microwave and serve cappuccino.

Saint Patrick's Day
Dinner for Six to Eight

Corned beef and cabbage are a natural choice for a party with an Irish theme. The corned beef, potatoes and vegetables are hearty fare, so for a refreshing change, the cabbage in this menu is served as a salad.

Menu

Confetti Slaw
Creamy cole slaw accented with bits of green pepper and tomato, page 130

Soda Bread
A round, raisin-stuffed loaf, page 136

Corned Beef & Vegetables
Served with horseradish sauce and a selection of mustards, page 93

Grasshopper Pie
Creamy, mint-green refrigerator pie, page 140

Irish Coffee
page 89

Preparation can be spread over several days, leaving little to do on the day of the party and nothing that demands last-minute attention. Start the meat about 3 hours before serving time. After standing, which is needed to complete cooking, the meat can be kept warm up to 45 minutes, making the schedule very flexible.

Use green mats of inexpensive fabric or construction paper with a white cloth under them, if you like. For a centerpiece, choose shamrock plants or greens.

Time Management

One or 2 days before the party, microwave soda bread. Cool completely; wrap.

The day before or early in the day, make cole slaw. Cover and refrigerate. Prepare Grasshopper Pie. It must be started at least 6 hours before serving to allow time for cooling and chilling.

About 3 hours before serving time, start corned beef. It should stand 10 to 20 minutes after microwaving, but can wait 30 to 45 minutes. Carve meat against the grain at a 45° angle in thin slices. Arrange on platter surrounded with vegetables.

After dessert, microwave Irish coffee while clearing the table.

Easter
Dinner for Eight

This festive menu features lamb, asparagus and new potatoes, which are at the peak of flavor and availability in the spring.

Begin the meal with a light and delicate soup; serve it as a first course while you are cooking the asparagus.

The timing for this meal depends on how you wish the lamb done. If you want the meat well done, start the soup about an hour and a half before serving time. With rare meat, allow about an hour. In either case, you will have time to shred the escarole and clean the asparagus and potatoes while the meat is microwaving.

Arrange the centerpiece in a shallow basket or use a plate as a base. Make a nest of clean, well-dried curly endive. For contrast of color and texture, add outer leaves from the escarole. Tuck decorated Easter eggs into the nest.

Menu

Escarole Soup
Shredded escarole in light chicken broth, page 87

Spiced Pear Salad
Saucy pears garnished with nut-covered cheese balls, page 131

Lemony Asparagus
page 109

Lamb Roast
page 99

New Potatoes
page 115

Assorted Bakery Rolls

Easter Cake
Decorated as an Easter basket, page 145

Time Management

Two days before Easter, prepare spiced pears. Cover and refrigerate.

The day before, microwave and frost cake. Cover loosely with foil, taking care not to touch frosting.

Early in the day, prepare cheese balls. Cover tightly and refrigerate. Conventionally hard cook eggs for asparagus garnish.

About 1½ hours before serving time, microwave seasoned soup stock while you prepare lamb for roasting.

When stock is very hot, set aside, covered, but do not add escarole. Microwave lamb until internal temperature reaches desired doneness. Tent loosely with foil.

While lamb is cooking, shred escarole, prepare potatoes and asparagus for microwaving and chop egg for garnish.

Reheat soup stock at High 3 to 5 minutes. Add escarole. Set aside, covered, until ready to serve.

Microwave potatoes while you assemble salads and place them on the table. Let potatoes stand, covered. They will stay hot for 20 minutes. Microwave asparagus while serving soup to guests. When asparagus is ready, serve with potatoes and lamb. Carve the meat at the table or just before serving.

Mother's Day
Breakfast for Four

Pamper Mom on Mother's Day by serving her breakfast in bed. This special occasion breakfast can be microwaved by Dad and the junior cooks.

Serve Mother's breakfast on a tray with a small bouquet of flowers. Cover the tray with a quilted place mat to keep the dishes from shifting as they are carried to her bedside.

The recipes make enough food for the whole family. Set up a card table in the bedroom where Dad and the children can join in the breakfast party.

Microwave cooking means easy cleanup — but don't leave the dishes in the sink.

Menu

Baked Grapefruit
Grapefruit halves topped with sour cream, brown sugar and cherries, page 125

Orange Breakfast Ring
Warm coffee cake with orange butter cream, page 137

Egg & Sausage Bake
Festive breakfast dish of eggs, sausage and cheese, page 107

Time Management

About 45 minutes to an hour before serving time, microwave the Orange Breakfast Ring.

Chop the onion and green pepper and combine with crumbled sausage.

Set the coffee ring aside, directly on the counter. While microwaving sausage, beat the eggs, milk and seasonings together.

While the eggs are cooking, drain sausage and spread it in baking dish. Don't overcook the eggs; they should be set but still soft.

Combine eggs and cheese; pour over sausage. Microwave the Egg & Sausage Bake while you section the grapefruit and hollow out the orange cup. While the eggs stand, heat the grapefruit. Invert the coffee ring onto a serving plate and decorate with the orange half filled with orange butter.

Father's Day
Dinner for Four to Six

For Father's Day, serve a man-pleasing meal of meat and potatoes. Make it a special occasion with his favorite, roast beef. Timing for the meal depends on how well he likes his roast beef done.

Estimate the time needed to microwave the meat to removal temperature. The meat must stand 10 to 20 minutes to complete cooking, but a roast weighing 4 pounds will keep warm an additional 20 to 40 minutes, giving you time to microwave potatoes and carrots.

As a centerpiece for the table, use gifts. Have each family member make a personal card.

Menu

Standing Rib Roast
page 91

Carrot Noodles
Carrot shavings in butter, page 112

Onion Caraway Bread
Wheat caraway bread with onion coating, page 137

Buttered Potato Wedges
Potatoes with Parmesan cheese
and green onion, page 115

Pecan Pie
page 139

Time Management

Early in the day, prepare and microwave pastry shell for pecan pie. Fill and microwave again. Refrigerate.

Microwave caraway bread. After standing, remove from dish, and cool. While bread is baking, peel and shave the carrots. Let stand at room temperature in a bowl of cool water.

About 1 to 1½ hours before serving time, remove pie from refrigerator and start roast. When roast is almost done, peel potatoes, cut into wedges and arrange on plate or microwave baking sheet. Tent roast with foil and let stand. While microwaving potatoes, drain carrots and prepare Carrot Noodles. Microwave while potatoes stand.

Fourth of July
Picnic for Twelve

On the Fourth of July, some people head for picnic tables in the park; others carry their own folding tables and chairs, while others spread a blanket on the beach or under a shady tree. You may choose the casual convenience of disposable plates, cups and tableware transported in a shopping bag, or travel in style with a hamper packed with picnic accessories. In either case, picnic equipment can be packed and ready to go well in advance. Make sure you bring any utensils you may need.

Plastic storage boxes in varying sizes are convenient for picnics because they stack neatly and have tightly sealed lids. An ice bucket with a removable plastic liner is ideal for transporting potato salad. To keep well-chilled food cool en route, pack the containers in an ice chest or styrofoam carriers.

If you don't have a cooler, improvise insulation by wrapping each container in foil, then several thicknesses of newspaper. Pack in cardboard boxes and keep cold.

All the food for this picnic is served cold. Some of it can be microwaved in advance. The hard cooked eggs are cooked conventionally. Buy the eggs several days before you plan to cook them because they are easier to shell when a few days old.

Menu

Deviled Eggs

Chipped Beef Dip
Creamy dip with crackers or tortilla chips, page 80

Fresh Zucchini Dip
Served with crisp vegetable dippers, page 80

Cold Fried Chicken
page 104

Creamy Potato Salad
page 132

Tomato Aspic
Tangy molded salad, page 133

Festive Gelatin Cake
White cake marbled with colorful gelatin, page 144

Time Management

Two days before the picnic, prepare tomato aspic. Leave in the mold for transporting to the picnic site.

The day before, microwave potatoes for salad. While hot, toss with Italian dressing and ¼ cup water. Cover and refrigerate.

Prepare chicken. Refrigerate, uncovered, until cool, then wrap in foil or pack in covered container. Refrigerate.

Make beef dip; pack in portable container. Refrigerate. Hard cook eggs conventionally. Prepare and pack tightly in shallow baking pan. Cover and refrigerate.

Prepare raw vegetables for dippers. Place in bowl of water to crisp. Cover and refrigerate.

Early in the day, microwave dressing for salad. Refrigerate until chilled.

Microwave and frost cakes. Cover dishes loosely with foil. Refrigerate. Mix cream into chilled dressing. Drain potatoes and complete salad. Pack in covered container or plastic liner of ice bucket. Chill.

Prepare zucchini dip. Pack in portable container. Refrigerate.

Just before leaving, drain vegetable dippers. Pack in plastic bag. Pack containers of food in ice chest or styrofoam carriers.

Labor Day
Barbecue for Ten to Twelve

Team the microwave oven and your grill for an end of the summer barbecue. Partial cooking by microwaves assures that the meat will be tender and fully cooked when it comes off the grill.

To finish the meat, prepare the coals or fire, then grill the meat basting with barbecue sauce for about half the conventional grilling time, until

Menu

Zucchini Slaw
Threads of zucchini, cabbage and carrot in sweet and sour dressing, page 130

Corn on the Cob
Served with herb butter, page 113

Barbecued Ribs or Chicken
Finished on the grill, page 95 or 104

Baked Beans
page 109

Pickles & Relish

Apple Cake
Honey-frosted fresh fruit cake, page 143

the internal temperature is 170° to 185°F.

Corn in the husk is easy to microwave. It must stand 5 minutes, but will stay hot for an additional 20 minutes. Serve it in a pail or large flower pot to double as a table centerpiece. Provide trash bags near the table for discarded husks. Husks and silk will strip off easily. A new

1-in. paint brush makes a good tool for applying the herb butter.

Finger foods like ribs and corn on the cob demand durable, absorbent napkins. Small terry towels are ideal. If you don't want to use your guest towels, buy a supply of seconds from a variety or discount store.

Time Management

Two days before, prepare barbecue sauce. Cover and refrigerate. Soak beans overnight.

The day before, prepare cake and frosting. Microwave beans. Frost cake; cover loosely with foil. Refrigerate beans.

Early in the day, prepare cabbage, carrot and onion for slaw. Refrigerate in separate plastic bags.

Microwave ribs or chicken. Cover; refrigerate.

Start charcoal fire in advance to prepare a good bed of coals. Complete cooking meat.

About 1 to 1¼ hours before serving time, reheat beans, covered, at High 18 to 25 minutes, stirring 3 or 4 times. Set aside covered; they will stay hot 1 hour.

Microwave 4 ears of corn at a time. Let stand in flower pot. While corn is cooking, shred zucchini for slaw.

Microwave dressing for slaw. Toss salad while heating herb butter. Serve the meal and continue to microwave corn. It's so good, you will probably want to cook more for seconds.

Halloween
Dinner for Twelve

The menu for this children's Halloween party is designed to provide nourishing, fun-to-eat food. The gelatin molded salad is decorated to resemble a jack-o'-lantern and serve as a table centerpiece. The caramel apples double as place cards and dessert with molasses cookies.

In addition there are popcorn balls, distributed as the children leave for a take-home treat.

Have a supply of chocolate-covered marshmallows ready to give trick-or-treaters who knock at the door.

Cover your table with brown wrapping paper and decorate with crepe paper streamers. Orange and black balloons, hanging from the ceiling or tied to the backs of chairs, add to the party atmosphere.

Take-home treat for guests:
Popcorn Balls, page 153

For trick-or-treaters at the door:
Chocolate Covered Marshmallows, page 152

Menu

Sloppy Joes
Perennial children's favorite, page 93

Jack-O'-Lantern Salad
Orange gelatin molded with crisp vegetables and decorated with a pumpkin face, page 135

Caramel Apples
Place card dessert, page 151

Molasses Cookies
page 147

Hot Spiced Cider
Honey-sweetened and garnished with oranges, page 87

Time Management

Three days before the party, make popcorn balls; cool. Wrap each one separately.

Two days before, microwave molasses cookies. When cool, store in a tightly covered plastic container.

The day before, combine ingredients for spiced cider. Microwave until sugar dissolves. Cover and refrigerate.

Prepare Jack-O'-Lantern Salad. Make chocolate covered marshmallows; wrap pieces in plastic.

Early in the day, write the name of each guest on a caramel apple stick using crayon or indelible marker. Coat apples with caramel and candy sprinkles. Set aside on wax paper.

About 45 minutes to an hour before serving time, microwave vegetables and ground beef for sloppy joes. Set aside.

Microwave spiced cider at High 20 to 25 minutes, or until very hot but not boiling. Add sauce ingredients to sloppy joe mixture. Cut orange wedges to garnish cider.

Microwave meat mixture while you arrange hamburger buns on serving plate. Strain cider into mugs and garnish with orange.

Thanksgiving
Dinner for Twelve to Fourteen

You really can cook Thanksgiving dinner for 12 to 14 people in your microwave oven. The dessert, cranberry relish and corn bread are prepared the day before so they can chill or cool. Some preparation can also be done early in the day. Many of these dishes have long standing and holding times, which you can use to microwave another food. The menu includes traditional Thanksgiving favorites, but the pie has a modern touch with a creamy blend of pumpkin and ice cream.

Choose a tablecloth or mats and napkins in harvest colors. Keep the centerpiece small so there will be plenty of room on the table for the food. Select fresh, well-shaped fall vegetables and shine them lightly with vegetable oil. Arrange in a basket, bowl or on a tray. Add a few unshelled nuts, stems of wheat and pheasant feathers. (Continued on following page)

Roast the turkey by time, not temperature, until the legs move freely and juices run clear. Then, as an added test for doneness, use a meat thermometer to check the internal temperature in several places, especially the meatiest part of the thighs and the breast.

Menu

Turkey
page 102

Corn Bread Dressing
page 137

Sweet Potato Casserole
Mashed sweet potatoes with orange and a hint of brandy, page 117

Cranberry-Orange Relish
page 126

Assorted Pickles & Olives

Green Bean Casserole
French-style beans with creamy sauce and crunchy toasted almonds, page 110

Assorted Bakery Rolls

Frosty Pumpkin Pie
Creamy blend of pumpkin and ice cream in a gingersnap crust, page 140

Time Management

The day before, prepare and freeze 2 pies. Microwave corn bread for dressing. Cool, cube and store in plastic bags.

Prepare and refrigerate cranberry relish.

Microwave sweet potatoes. Let stand until cool. Leave in jackets and refrigerate.

Early in the day, microwave almond garnish for beans. Prepare cream sauce for beans. Cover and refrigerate. Microwave bacon and vegetables for dressing. Drain bacon on paper towels. Set vegetables aside, covered.

About 2½ to 3 hours before serving time, microwave sweet potatoes 2 to 4 minutes at High to remove chill. Start microwaving turkey. Peel sweet potatoes and mash with butter. Combine with remaining ingredients.

When turkey legs move freely and juices run clear, check internal temperature in several places with meat thermometer. Continue microwaving until internal temperature reaches 170°F., then wrap loosely with foil and let stand.

Microwave sweet potatoes as directed, but increase final heating time to 9 to 15 minutes. Garnish, if desired, cover with foil and set aside. Potatoes will stay hot 45 minutes.

Combine vegetables for corn bread dressing with bacon, broth, water and seasonings. Microwave at High 1 to 3 minutes to heat before continuing as directed in the recipe. Set aside, covered.

While you microwave green beans, arrange covered foods and cranberry relish on table. When beans are done, reheat cream sauce at High 2 to 4 minutes, stirring once or twice. Pour sauce over drained beans, garnish with almonds. Remove foil from turkey, sweet potatoes and dressing and serve.

After the meal, remove pies from freezer. If too firm to cut, microwave each at 50% (Medium) 15 to 30 seconds to soften slightly.

Holiday Make-Aheads

Early in the holiday season make a supply of Christmas goodies to serve or give as gifts. The confections shown here keep well, so they can be made in advance and stored at room temperature. Package them in decorative containers to enhance a gift or add to the festive appearance of your home. In a glass jar with a tight fitting lid, the food itself provides the decorative element. Cover coffee cans with calico prints or adhesive shelf paper. Wrap single cookies or candies in plastic wrap tied with a yarn bow; place them in a bowl or hang them on the Christmas tree for individual treats.

Pictured clockwise: Chocolate Bourbon Balls, page 152, Buttermilk Pralines, page 152, Coconut Date Balls, page 153, Chocolate Covered Marshmallows, page 152 and Thin Mint Layers, page 153. Not pictured: Sesame Bars, page 147 and Fruitcake Cookies, page 147.

Trim the Tree
Party for Ten to Twelve

Gather your friends 'round the wassail bowl while they help trim the Christmas tree or invite neighbors in for a warm-up after caroling. Wassail is a traditional way to toast the holiday season. If you prefer a non-alcoholic beverage serve hot spiced cider.

The food is prepared in advance. At serving time, heat the punch and crab appetizers and garnish the cold dishes.

Set food and punch out on a table near the Christmas tree, so guests can enjoy them while they hang the ornaments and lights.

Use a mat or runner under the wassail bowl to protect the table from heat and spills. As a seasonal decoration for the table, cover a shoe box with shiny foil. Attach two long candy canes to the bottom for runners. Fill the "sleigh" with holly and pine cones. Tuck in small, gaily wrapped packages. These might be thank-you favors for your guests, perhaps small ornaments they can take home to hang on their own trees.

Menu

Pickled Sausages
Spiced pearl onions and knockwurst chunks, page 84

Crab-Stuffed Zucchini
Creamed crab in hollowed zucchini slices, page 82

Chicken Liver Pâté
Molded pâté garnished with chopped tomato and cucumber, page 84

Cheese Ball
Zippy blend of three cheeses, page 81

Pumpernickel Party Slices & Crackers

Wassail or Hot Spiced Cider
Traditional hot punch, page 87

Time Management

Five to 7 days in advance, pickle sausages and onions. Cover and refrigerate.

One or 2 days in advance, mix and shape cheese ball. Wrap in plastic wrap. Refrigerate.

The day before, prepare liver pâté. Pour into oiled mold. Cover and refrigerate. Microwave crab stuffing. Cover and refrigerate.

Slice and hollow out zucchini cups. Refrigerate in plastic bag.

Early in the day of the party, chop pecans for cheese ball. Set aside. Prepare tomato and cucumber garnish for pâté, if desired. Refrigerate separately in plastic bags.

Slice lemons or oranges for wassail. Refrigerate, covered. Pat zucchini cups dry with paper towels. Arrange on 2 paper towel-lined plates. Fill with crab mixture. Cover with plastic wrap; refrigerate.

About half an hour before serving time, mix and microwave wassail. While punch is heating, unwrap cheese ball, roll in pecans and place on cheese board or plate.

Unmold pâté onto serving plate and garnish. Arrange breads and crackers for serving. Drain pickled sausages. Rinse in cool water if necessary to remove fat. Uncover zucchini cups and sprinkle with paprika.

When wassail is heated, stir in bourbon and garnish with fruit slices. Microwave first plate of zucchini cups at 70% (Medium-High) 2 to 5 minutes, or until heated, rotating once or twice. Serve wassail and appetizers; microwave second plate of zucchini as needed.

Christmas Eve
Dinner for Six to Eight

Plum pudding is a Christmas tradition which many conventional cooks avoid because it requires hours of steaming, frequent checking of water level and lengthy reheating. Microwave cooks can steam a pudding in less than 20 minutes and reheat it in a minute or two.

The secret of serving this colorful meal without fuss is to make use of standing and holding times. While the first food is in the oven, get the second ready to cook, then microwave it while the first one is standing. Foods with long holding times are cooked first and will stay hot while you microwave the remaining dishes.

Set your table with a simple red cloth and white china. For a centerpiece, fill a large goblet with Christmas baubles of red silk or clear glass. To provide a candlestick for each guest, core well-polished apples and insert small tapers. Decorate with sprigs of holly.

Menu

Pineapple Cheese Salad
Fruits and nuts in creamy lime gelatin, page 134

Minted Carrots & Brussels Sprouts
page 112

Fruited Pork Roast
Boneless pork baked with classic sauce of dried fruits, page 97

Twice Baked Potatoes
page 117

Dickens' Plum Pudding
An English tradition with hard sauce, page 149

Time Management

The day before, prepare and refrigerate gelatin salad.

Early in the day, microwave plum pudding. Set aside, covered. Mix and microwave fruit sauce for pork roast. Set aside.

About 1½ to 2 hours before serving time, microwave bacon for twice baked potatoes. Drain, crumble and set aside.

Microwave potatoes. Wrap in foil to keep hot until time to mash.

Cook roast while you julienne carrots. Set out butter to soften for hard sauce.

When the internal temperature of the roast reaches 165°F., spoon on remaining fruit

sauce, tent loosely with foil and let stand. Internal temperature will rise to 170°F. and roast will keep warm until serving time.

Microwave onion and butter for mashed potatoes, then microwave Brussels sprouts and carrots. While vegetables are cooking, mash potatoes and stuff shells. Melt butter with mint and pour over drained vegetables.

Microwave potatoes at High 3 to 7 minutes, while you unmold the salad. If necessary, reheat vegetables at High 1 to 2 minutes.

After the meal, invert plum pudding on microwave oven-safe serving plate. Microwave at High 1 to 2 minutes while preparing hard sauce.

Christmas Day
Dinner for Six to Eight

Christmas dinner should be festive but not fussy. The food for this ample menu is easy to prepare, so you won't be tied to the kitchen every moment while it's cooking. Use the signal on your microwave oven to tell you when it's time to rotate a dish, glaze the ham or put another food in the oven.

The holiday centerpiece is made from a 1-lb.

coffee can and 6-in. candy canes (40 to 45). Arrange the candy canes upright around the can, with their curved ends outward. Use a large rubber band or length of florist wire to hold them in place. Tie a bright Christmas ribbon over the rubber band and fill the container with evergreens or holly.

Menu

Parmesan Lettuce Wedges
Dressed with Parmesan vinaigrette, page 129

Green Beans & Broccoli
page 110

Apricot-Glazed Ham
page 98

Glazed Onions
A hint of mustard in the sweet and sour sauce, page 114

Fruit-Filled Squash Rings
Acorn squash with cranberry, apple and nut stuffing, page 117

Mincemeat Pie
page 141

Time Management

The day before, prepare mincemeat pie. Cool and refrigerate.

About 1½ to 2 hours before serving time, remove pie from refrigerator. Let stand at room temperature. Microwave acorn squash. Combine ingredients for cranberry filling and peel and quarter onions. Set squash aside to stand. Microwave cranberry mixture. Set aside to cool.

Prepare sweet and sour onions. After cooking they will keep warm for an hour. Microwave ham, glazing as directed in recipe. While ham is cooking, prepare salad ingredients. Refrigerate lettuce wedges until serving time.

Tent ham with foil and let stand. While you microwave beans and broccoli, cut and seed squash. Place rings on microwave baking sheet. Cover with plastic wrap.

Set beans and broccoli aside, covered. Microwave squash at High 4 to 7 minutes. Arrange lettuce wedges on salad plates.

Place squash rings on serving plate; fill with cranberry sauce and serve dinner.

After the meal, you can serve pie at room temperature, or warmed in the microwave at 70% (Medium-High) 4 to 8 minutes.

Recipes

Appetizers

Shrimp in Beer ▼
Freezer Cocktail Party, page 32

2 pkgs. (12 oz. each) frozen
   quick-cooking shrimp
1 can (12 oz.) beer
1 teaspoon garlic powder
1 teaspoon chopped chives

Serves 10 to 12

Combine all ingredients in 2-qt.
casserole; cover. Microwave at
High 8 to 13 minutes, or until
shrimp are opaque, stirring 2 or
3 times. Drain all but ½ cup
liquid before serving. Serve with
cocktail picks.

Spiced Shrimp
New Year's Eve, page 46

2 lbs. raw shrimp, peeled and
   deveined
¼ cup butter or margarine
2 tablespoons all-purpose
   flour
2 teaspoons snipped fresh
   parsley or 1 teaspoon
   dried parsley flakes

½ teaspoon ground coriander
½ teaspoon ground cumin
¼ teaspoon salt
¼ teaspoon pepper
¼ teaspoon ground nutmeg
⅛ teaspoon ground cloves
1¼ cups milk

Serves 6 to 8

Place shrimp in 1½-qt. casserole. Microwave, covered, at High 5
to 8 minutes, or until shrimp are opaque, stirring 2 or 3 times. Do
not overcook. Set aside.

Place butter in 4-cup measure. Microwave at High 45 to 60
seconds, or until melted. Blend in flour, parsley, coriander, cumin,
salt, pepper, nutmeg and cloves. Blend in milk. Microwave at High
3 to 6 minutes, or until thick and bubbly, stirring with wire whip 2 or
3 times. Drain shrimp; stir in sauce. Serve with cocktail picks.

Polynesian Appetizers ▼
Freezer Impromptu Dinner, page 28

1 tablespoon packed brown
    sugar
2 teaspoons cornstarch
⅛ teaspoon ground ginger
⅛ teaspoon garlic powder
1 tablespoon water
1 tablespoon soy sauce
1 can (8¼ oz.) pineapple
    chunks, drained and ⅓
    cup juice reserved
½ pkg. (8 oz.) frozen fully
    cooked brown and
    serve sausages

Serves 2

In 1-qt. casserole blend brown
sugar, cornstarch, ginger, garlic
powder, water, soy sauce and
pinneapple juice. Cut each
sausage into thirds. Stir into
casserole with pineapple
chunks. Microwave at High 3 to
7 minutes, or until sauce is
thickened, stirring 2 or 3 times.

Shrimp Wrap-Ups ▲
Midnight Supper, page 26

8 slices bacon
8 large raw shrimp, peeled,
    deveined and cut in half
1 large green pepper, cut into
    16 pieces
2 tablespoons soy sauce

2 tablespoons white wine or
    water
2 tablespoons chili sauce
2 tablespoons plum or grape
    jelly

Serves 6

Place 3 layers of paper towel directly on oven floor. Arrange 4
bacon slices on towel; cover with another towel. Arrange remaining
4 bacon slices on top; cover with towel. Microwave at High 4 to 5
minutes, or until bacon is slightly brown but not fully cooked.

Cut bacon slices in half. Wrap a piece of shrimp and green
pepper in each bacon piece. Secure with a cocktail pick. Place in
9 × 9-in. glass baking dish.

In 2-cup measure mix remaining ingredients. Pour over wrap-ups.
Cover. Refrigerate no longer than 8 hours or overnight, stirring
once or twice. To serve, microwave at High 3 to 4 minutes, or until
shrimp is cooked.

Fresh Zucchini Dip

Fourth of July, page 60

Pictured above, upper left

1½ cups shredded zucchini
    (1 medium)
¼ cup finely chopped onion
¼ cup finely chopped green
    pepper
  1 tablespoon butter or
    margarine
¼ cup mayonnaise or salad
    dressing
¾ cup dairy sour cream
  1 teaspoon garlic salt
  1 teaspoon Worcestershire
    sauce
    Dash cayenne

Makes 2 cups

Place shredded zucchini
between layers of paper towel.
Press to remove excess
moisture. In 1-qt. casserole
combine onion, green pepper
and butter. Microwave at High 1
to 3 minutes, or until onion is
tender. Stir in zucchini and
remaining ingredients. Chill at
least 2 hours.

Chipped Beef Dip

Fourth of July, page 60

Pictured above, lower left

¼ cup chopped green onion
  1 clove garlic, minced
  1 tablespoon butter or
    margarine
  1 pkg. (8 oz.) cream cheese
½ cup dairy sour cream
¼ cup half and half or milk
  1 pkg. (2½ oz.) dried beef,
    chopped
  2 tablespoons snipped fresh
    parsley
  1 tablespoon prepared
    horseradish
  1 tablespoon lemon juice

Makes about 2 cups

In 1-qt. casserole combine
green onion, garlic and butter.
Microwave at High 30 to 60
seconds, or until butter melts.
Add cream cheese. Microwave
at High 45 seconds to 1½
minutes, or until cream cheese
is softened. Mix in remaining
ingredients. Chill at least 2
hours or overnight.

Jalapeño Cheese Dip

After the Game, page 22

Pictured above, upper right

  1 medium onion, chopped
  1 tablespoon vegetable oil
  2 cups shredded Monterey
    Jack cheese
  2 cups shredded Cheddar
    cheese
½ cup half and half
  2 tablespoons chopped
    jalapeño peppers

Serves 10 to 12

Place onion and oil in 1½-qt.
casserole. Cover. Microwave at
High 2 to 3 minutes, or until
onion is tender. Stir in remaining
ingredients. Reduce power to
50% (Medium). Microwave 3 to
6 minutes, or until heated and
smooth, stirring every 2 minutes.
Serve with taco chips, if desired.

Curry Dip

New Year's Eve, page 46

Pictured opposite, lower right

1 pkg. (8 oz.) cream cheese
3 tablespoons milk
½ teaspoon curry powder
½ teaspoon garlic salt
1 cup dairy sour cream
8 to 10 cups raw vegetables
(carrot and celery sticks,
cauliflowerets, broccoli
flowerets, zucchini strips)

Serves 6 to 8

Place cream cheese in small
bowl. Microwave at High 20 to
45 seconds, or until softened.
Mix in milk, curry powder and
garlic salt. Microwave at High
30 to 60 seconds, or until warm.
Stir to blend. Mix in sour cream.
Serve with raw vegetables.

Advance preparation: Prepare
the day before or the morning
of the party. Cover and refrigerate. Before serving, microwave
dip at High 45 seconds to 1½
minutes, or until softened,
stirring once or twice. Add 1 to
2 teaspoons milk if needed for
smoother consistency.

Cheese Ball

Trim the Tree, page 70

Pictured below

¼ cup chopped green pepper
¼ cup chopped green onion
1 teaspoon butter or margarine
1 pkg. (8 oz.) cream cheese
2 cups shredded Cheddar
cheese
1 pkg. (4 oz.) blue cheese,
crumbled
1 tablespoon chopped pimiento
2 teaspoons prepared
horseradish
2 teaspoons Worcestershire
sauce
1 clove garlic, minced
½ cup chopped pecans

Serves 10 to 12

In small bowl combine green
pepper, onion and butter; cover.
Microwave at High 30 to 45
seconds, or until vegetables are
tender-crisp, stirring once. Place
cream cheese in large bowl.
Reduce power to 50% (Medium).
Microwave 1 to 1½ minutes, or
until softened. Stir in vegetables
and remaining ingredients
except pecans. Shape into ball.
Wrap in plastic wrap. Chill 2 to
3 hours. Unwrap; roll in pecans.
Serve with assorted crackers,
if desired.

Miniature Chicken Drumsticks

Freezer Cocktail Party, page 32

3 lbs. chicken wings
6 tablespoons butter or
margarine
1 cup finely crushed rich,
round crackers
2 tablespoons sesame seed
1 teaspoon paprika
½ teaspoon onion powder
½ teaspoon salt

Serves 10 to 12

Cut chicken wings at joints into
3 parts each; discard tip. Wash
thoroughly; pat dry. Melt butter
in pie plate at High 1 to 1½
minutes. Mix remaining
ingredients. Dip chicken into
butter, then roll in crumbs.
Place on baking sheet with
meatiest portions to outside of
dish. Microwave at High 10 to
16 minutes, or until juices run
clear, rearranging 2 or 3 times
but do not turn over. Cool.

Cover and freeze overnight on
baking sheet. Pack in freezer
container; label. Freeze no
longer than 2 weeks. To reheat,
place on baking sheet.
Microwave, uncovered, at High
11 to 15 minutes, or until hot,
rotating chicken 2 or 3 times.

◀ Crab-Stuffed Zucchini

Trim the Tree, page 70

- ¾ cup chopped fresh mushrooms
- 3 tablespoons butter or margarine
- 2 tablespoons all-purpose flour
- ¾ cup half and half
- ½ cup chopped green onion
- ¼ teaspoon paprika
- ¼ teaspoon salt
- ⅛ teaspoon pepper
- 2 tablespoons sherry
- 2 cans (6¾ oz. each) crab meat, rinsed, drained and cartilage removed
- 1¼ to 1½-lb. small zucchini, cut into ¾-in. pieces

Makes 4 to 4½ dozen

Advance preparation: Prepare recipe as directed below, but do not sprinkle with paprika. Cover each plate with plastic wrap. Refrigerate no longer than 8 hours. Uncover. Sprinkle with paprika. Microwave one plate at a time at 70% (Medium-High) 2 to 5 minutes, or until heated, rotating once or twice.

How to Microwave Crab-Stuffed Zucchini

Combine mushrooms and butter in 1-qt. casserole. Microwave at High 1 to 2 minutes, or until butter is melted and mushrooms are tender. Stir in flour. Blend in half and half until smooth. Stir in onion, paprika, salt, pepper and sherry.

Microwave at High 2 to 4 minutes, or until very thick, blending with wire whip once or twice. Stir in crab meat. Set aside. With a spoon, hollow out each zucchini piece about halfway down leaving ⅛ to ¼ inch on sides. Spoon crab mixture into zucchini pieces.

Place on two paper towel-lined plates. Sprinkle with additional paprika. Reduce power to 70% (Medium-High). Microwave one plate at a time 1 to 3 minutes, or until heated, rotating plate once or twice. Repeat with remaining plate.

Sausage Balls
Freezer Cocktail Party, page 32

1 pkg. (12 oz.) bulk pork
    sausage
¾ cup seasoned bread crumbs
¼ cup grated Parmesan
    cheese
⅛ teaspoon ground red pepper
1 tablespoon dried parsley
    flakes
2 eggs

Makes 4 dozen

Crumble sausage into 2-qt. casserole. Microwave at High 2 to 4 minutes, or until sausage is no longer pink, stirring to break apart; drain. Stir in remaining ingredients. Shape into balls, about 1 teaspoon each. Place on wax paper-lined baking sheet; cover. Freeze overnight. Pack in freezer container; label. Freeze no longer than 2 weeks.

To serve, place 24 balls around edge of paper towel-lined 12-in. serving plate. Microwave at High 1½ to 3½ minutes, or until heated and firm to the touch, rearranging once. Repeat with remaining sausage balls.

Spinach Balls
Freezer Cocktail Party, page 32

1 pkg. (10 oz.) frozen,
    chopped spinach
¾ cup shredded Swiss cheese
¼ cup dry bread crumbs
2 tablespoons grated
    Parmesan cheese
1 tablespoon grated onion
½ teaspoon salt
1 egg, beaten

Makes 2 dozen

Place package of spinach in oven. Microwave at High 4 to 5 minutes, or until defrosted. Drain, pressing out excess liquid. Mix with remaining ingredients. Shape into 1-in. balls, about 1½ teaspoons each. Place on wax paper-lined baking sheet; cover. Freeze overnight. Pack in freezer container; label. Freeze no longer than 2 weeks.

To serve, place all spinach balls on paper towel-lined baking sheet. Microwave at High 2 minutes. Reduce power to 50% (Medium). Microwave 4½ to 6 minutes, or until hot and just set, rearranging once or twice.

Ham Salad Finger Rolls
Freezer Cocktail Party, page 32

1 can (6½ oz.) chunked ham
¼ cup mayonnaise or salad
    dressing
2 tablespoons sweet pickle
    relish

1 teaspoon grated onion
6 slices whole-wheat bread
¼ cup butter or margarine
1 egg
¼ cup sesame seed

Makes 3 dozen

In small bowl mix ham, mayonnaise, pickle relish and onion. Set aside. Trim crusts from bread. Roll to ¼-in. thickness with rolling pin. Spread each with ham mixture; roll up jelly roll-style.

Place butter in shallow dish. Microwave at High 45 to 60 seconds, or until melted. Beat egg into butter. Roll sandwich rolls in butter-egg mixture, then in sesame seed to coat generously. Wrap, label and freeze. Freeze no longer than 2 weeks.

To serve, cut each roll into 6 pieces. Place around edges of two 12-in. plates. Microwave each plate at High 3 to 6 minutes, or until hot, rotating plate once or twice.

Spiced Nuts ▲
Spring Open House, page 20

¼ cup butter or margarine
2 tablespoons Worcestershire
    sauce
¾ teaspoon seasoned salt
½ teaspoon garlic powder
¼ teaspoon cayenne
2 cans (12 oz. each) mixed
    nuts

Makes 4 cups

Place butter in 3 qt. casserole. Microwave at High 45 to 60 seconds, or until melted. Mix in remaining ingredients except nuts. Add nuts, stirring to coat. Microwave at High 7 to 9 minutes, or until butter is absorbed, stirring 2 or 3 times during cooking. Spread on paper towel-lined baking sheet to dry. Store nuts in tightly covered container.

Florentine Canapés

New Year's Day, page 48

2 pkgs. (9 oz. each) frozen
    creamed spinach
¼ cup grated Parmesan
    cheese
¼ cup seasoned dry bread
    crumbs
¼ cup chopped tomato
2 teaspoons instant minced
    onion
⅛ to ¼ teaspoon ground
    nutmeg
    Melba cracker rounds

Makes 4 to 5 dozen

Place spinach in 2-qt. casserole.
Microwave at High 4 to 8
minutes, or until defrosted,
breaking apart with fork once or
twice. Drain. Stir in cheese,
bread crumbs, tomato, minced
onion and nutmeg. Spread on
crackers. Place 12 crackers on
paper towel-lined plate.
Microwave at High 1 to 1½
minutes, or until hot, rotating
plate once. Repeat with
remaining canapés.

Advance preparation: Prepare
spinach spread the day before.
Cover and refrigerate. Canapés
can be assembled 2 to 3 hours
in advance and refrigerated.
Add 15 to 20 seconds to microwaving time if spread is cold.

Crab Canapés

Freezer Cocktail Party, page 32

1 can (6½ oz.) crab meat,
    rinsed, drained and
    cartilage removed
⅓ cup all-purpose flour
1 egg
¼ cup finely chopped green
    onion
1 jar (2 oz.) chopped pimiento,
    drained
1 teaspoon lemon juice
1 teaspoon Worcestershire
    sauce
¼ teaspoon salt
⅛ teaspoon pepper
36 melba sesame rounds

Makes 3 dozen

Mix all ingredients except melba
rounds in medium bowl. Drop
by teaspoonfuls onto wax
paper-lined baking sheet. Cover
and freeze overnight. Pack in
freezer container; label. Freeze
no longer than 2 weeks.

To serve, place 18 melba
rounds around edge of paper
towel-lined 12-in. serving plate.
Top each with frozen crab
mixture. Microwave at 70%
(Medium-High) 1¾ to 3 minutes,
or until heated, rearranging after
half the time. Repeat with
remaining canapés as needed.

◄ Pickled Sausages

Trim the Tree, page 70

¾ cup sugar
1 teaspoon pickling spice
1 teaspoon salt
¼ teaspoon peppercorns
½ cup water
½ cup cider vinegar
1 lb. knockwurst or ring
    bologna
1½ cups pearl onions, or
    chunks of white onion

Serves 10 to 12

In 2-qt. casserole mix sugar,
pickling spice, salt, peppercorns, water and vinegar; cover.
Microwave at High 1 to 3
minutes, or until boiling. Cut
knockwurst lengthwise in half,
then cut into ½-in. pieces. Add
knockwurst and onions to
sugar-vinegar mixture; cover.
Refrigerate 4 to 7 days, stirring
occasionally. Remove
knockwurst and onions to
serving dish with slotted spoon.
Serve with cocktail picks.

Chicken Liver Pâté

Trim the Tree, page 70

1½ lbs. chicken livers
1 teaspoon instant chicken
    bouillon granules
½ cup water
1 hard cooked egg
¼ cup butter or margarine,
    softened
2 tablespoons finely chopped
    onion
1 clove garlic, minced
1 teaspoon salt
1 teaspoon dry mustard

Serves 10 to 12

In 1½-qt. casserole combine
chicken livers, bouillon granules
and water; cover. Microwave at
High 8 to 12 minutes, or until
livers are no longer pink, stirring
after half the time. Drain. Pureé
livers and egg in meat grinder
or food processor. In medium
bowl, blend pureé with
remaining ingredients. Pour into
well-oiled 2-cup mold. Chill at
least 6 hours or overnight.
Unmold onto serving plate.
Garnish with chopped tomatoes
and cucumbers, if desired.

Spinach-Filled Bread ▶

Cocktail Party Buffet, page 18

1 loaf (16 oz.) round crusty
    bread
2 pkgs. (10 oz. each) frozen
    chopped spinach
2 pkgs. (8 oz. each) cream
    cheese
3 tablespoons milk
1 teaspoon lemon juice
½ teaspoon salt
⅛ teaspoon pepper, optional
    Dash ground nutmeg

Serves 8

Advance preparation: Prepare
filling 1 day ahead; refrigerate.
To serve, microwave filling at
High 30 seconds to 1¼
minutes, or until warm. Fill
bread. Microwave as directed.

How to Microwave Spinach-Filled Bread

Cut 1½- to 2-in. slice from top
of bread. Cut a circle 1½
inches from outer edge of crust.

Remove center leaving at least
2 inches of bread on bottom.
Cut center and top into pieces
for dipping. Set aside.

Place packages of spinach in
oven. Microwave at High 4½ to
6½ minutes, or until heated,
rearranging once. Drain,
pressing out excess liquid.

Place cream cheese in medium
bowl. Microwave at High 30 to
45 seconds, or until softened.
Mix in remaining ingredients.

Spoon into bread shell. Place
on paper towel-lined plate.

Microwave at High 45 seconds
to 1¼ minutes, or until bread is
warm. Serve with bread pieces
for dipping.

85

Soups & Beverages

◄ Egg Drop Soup
Foreign Affair: Oriental, page 38

2 cans (10¾ oz. each)
   condensed chicken broth
6 cups hot water
2 teaspoons instant chicken
   bouillon granules
   Dash pepper
2 eggs, well beaten
⅓ cup diagonally sliced
   green onion

Serves 6 to 8

In 3-qt. casserole combine
broth, water, bouillon granules
and pepper; cover. Microwave
at High 7 to 11 minutes, or until
boiling. Pour eggs in thin stream
into soup, stirring in a circular
motion. Let stand, covered, 3
minutes. Sprinkle with green
onion before serving.

Advance preparation: Soup
can stand 30 to 35 minutes
before serving. Reheat at High
1 to 2 minutes, if needed.

Escarole Soup
Easter, page 54

3 cans (10¾ oz. each)
   condensed chicken broth
2½ cups hot water
1½ tablespoons lemon juice
2 teaspoons chopped chives
1 teaspoon sugar
⅛ teaspoon white pepper
2 cups shredded escarole

Serves 8

In 3-qt. casserole combine all
ingredients except escarole.
Cover. Microwave at High 10 to
15 minutes, or until very hot. Stir
in escarole.

Hot Spiced Cider
Halloween, page 64

12 cups apple cider, divided
¼ cup packed brown sugar
¼ cup honey
4 sticks cinnamon
1 teaspoon whole cloves
1 teaspoon whole allspice
12 orange wedges, studded
   with cloves, optional

Serves 12

In 4- or 5-qt. casserole combine
1 cup cider, the brown sugar
and honey. Microwave at High
1 to 2 minutes, or until sugar
dissolves. Add remaining cider,
cinnamon, cloves and allspice;
cover. Refrigerate 8 hours.

To reheat, microwave at High
20 to 25 minutes, or until hot,
stirring after half the cooking
time. Do not boil. Let stand,
covered, 5 minutes. Strain. Pour
into mugs or cups. Garnish
each with orange wedge.

Wassail
Trim the Tree, page 70

6 cups apple cider
2 cups orange juice
1 cup lemonade
½ cup sugar
1 teaspoon instant tea
   powder
1 teaspoon chopped
   crystallized ginger
10 whole cloves
2 sticks cinnamon
1½ to 2 cups bourbon

Serves 10 to 12

In large bowl combine all
ingredients except bourbon.
Cover with plastic wrap.
Microwave at High 12 to 15
minutes, or until desired serving
temperature, stirring every 5
minutes. Stir in bourbon.
Garnish with orange or lemon
slices, if desired.

◀ Fruit Punch in
Watermelon Bowl
Spring Open House, page 20

1 large oblong watermelon
1 large cantaloupe
3 cups sugar
3 cups hot water
2 qts. strawberries, divided
1 cup cranberry cocktail juice
   Juice of 5 oranges
   Juice of 5 lemons
2 qts. carbonated water
2 to 3 cups crushed ice

Serves 20

How to Microwave Fruit Punch in Watermelon Bowl

Cut slice from bottom of watermelon to keep it from tipping. Cut off top third. Scoop balls; remove seeds. Cover and refrigerate balls. Remove remaining pulp from bottom with large spoon to form bowl.

Cut scallops or a saw-tooth design using a small glass or bowl as guide for a decorative edge. Drain shell. Refrigerate.

Scoop balls from cantaloupe. Cover; refrigerate. Combine sugar and hot water in 2-qt. casserole; cover. Microwave at High 9 to 12 minutes, or until boiling. Uncover. Microwave at High 4 minutes. Cool.

Remove hulls from 1-qt. strawberries. In 5-qt. casserole combine hulled strawberries, cranberry, orange and lemon juices and cooled syrup. Chill.

Rub rims of 20 glasses with orange or lemon rind, then dip in additional sugar. Place a whole strawberry on each rim. Chill until sugar is hardened.

Pour carbonated water, ice and juice mixture into watermelon bowl just before serving. Serve in sugar-frosted glasses. Combine watermelon and cantaloupe balls to serve separately.

Irish Coffee ▲

Saint Patrick's Day, page 52

¼ cup packed light brown
   sugar
2 tablespoons plus 1
   teaspoon instant coffee
   crystals
5½ cups hot water
1¼ to 1½ cups Irish whiskey
   Sweetened whipped cream

Serves 6 to 8

In 2-qt. measure or bowl
combine brown sugar, coffee
crystals and hot water; cover.
Microwave at High 5 to 8
minutes, or until very hot. Stir to
dissolve brown sugar. Stir in
whiskey. Pour into individual
cups. Top with sweetened
whipped cream.

Cappuccino for Two ▲

Valentine's Day, page 50

2 to 3 teaspoons packed light
   brown sugar
2 teaspoons instant coffee
   crystals
1⅓ cups hot water
   ¼ cup orange liqueur
   Sweetened whipped cream

Serves 2

In 2-cup measure combine
brown sugar, coffee crystals,
and hot water. Cover.
Microwave at High 2 to 4
minutes, or until hot. Stir to
dissolve sugar. Stir in liqueur.
Pour into individual cups. Top
with sweetened whipped cream.

Cappuccino for Eight

Foreign Affair: Italian, page 40

2 to 3 tablespoons packed
   light brown sugar
2 tablespoons instant coffee
   crystals
4 cups hot water
¾ cup orange liqueur
   Sweetened whipped cream

Serves 8

In 1½- to 2-qt. measure or bowl
combine brown sugar, coffee
crystals and hot water. Cover.
Microwave at High 4 to 6½
minutes, or until hot. Stir to
dissolve sugar. Stir in liqueur.
Pour into individual cups. Top
with sweetened whipped cream.

Meats

◄ Standing Rib Roast

Father's Day, page 58

4 lb. beef standing rib roast

Serves 4 to 6

Place roast fat side down on roasting rack. Estimate total cooking time using desired doneness as guide. Divide total time in half. Microwave at High 8 minutes. Reduce power to 50% (Medium). Microwave remainder of first half of total time.

Turn roast fat side up. Insert microwave thermometer, if desired. Microwave at 50% (Medium) the second half of time, or until desired internal temperature. Let stand 10 to 20 minutes, tented loosely with foil.

Desired Doneness	Min./lb.	Removal Temp.
Rare	9 to 12	120°F.
Medium	10 to 14	135°F.
Well	11 to 15	150°F.

Sirloin Teriyaki

Cocktail Party Buffet, page 18

½ cup soy sauce
¼ cup sherry
3 tablespoons honey
¼ teaspoon minced gingerroot or ⅛ teaspoon ground ginger
⅛ to ¼ teaspoon garlic powder
2 lbs. boneless beef sirloin steak, cut into thin strips
1 tablespoon cornstarch

Serves 8

In medium bowl combine soy sauce, sherry, honey, gingerroot and garlic powder. Microwave at High 1 minute. Stir; add steak strips. Cover and refrigerate 8 hours or overnight, stirring once or twice if marinade doesn't cover all of the meat.

Drain marinade into 9-in. round cake dish. Blend in cornstarch. Stir in steak strips. Microwave at High 8½ to 11 minutes, or until meat is cooked, stirring once or twice. Garnish with chopped green onions, if desired.

Pepper Steak
Freezer Impromptu Dinner, page 28

2 tablespoons butter or
  margarine
¾ lb. beef boneless top sirloin
  steak, cut into thin strips
1 large green pepper, cut into
  ½-in. strips
1 cup sliced fresh mushrooms

3 green onions, cut into ¾-in.
  pieces
1 small clove garlic, minced
2 tablespoons soy sauce
1 tablespoon cornstarch
2 tablespoons water

Serves 2

In 2-qt. casserole microwave butter at High 30 to 60 seconds, or
until melted. Stir in beef, green pepper, mushrooms, green onions,
garlic and soy sauce until coated. Microwave 4 to 6 minutes, or
until beef is no longer pink and peppers are heated, stirring once
or twice. Package, label and freeze up to 6 weeks.

To serve, remove from package and place in 1-qt. casserole.
Microwave at 70% (Medium-High), covered, 4 to 7 minutes, or until
food can be broken apart with fork. In 1-cup measure blend
cornstarch and water. Stir into beef mixture. Microwave, covered,
at 70% (Medium-High) 6 to 9 minutes, or until thickened and very
hot, stirring once or twice.

Sirloin Tip Roast ▲
Freezer Buffet, page 36

5 lb. frozen beef sirloin tip roast
2 tablespoons all-purpose flour
1 cup water
1 pkg. (1 oz.) au jus gravy mix

Serves 10 to 12

Place unwrapped frozen roast
on roasting rack. Cover with
wax paper. Microwave at High
5 minutes. Turn roast over;
cover. Microwave at High 5
minutes. Reduce power to 50%
(Medium). Microwave 30 minutes.
Turn over. Insert microwave
thermometer. Cover. Microwave
at 50% (Medium) 20 to 45
minutes, or until internal temperature reaches 125°F. Let stand
10 minutes, tented with foil.

Reserve ⅓ cup drippings. In
medium bowl blend flour into
water. Stir in reserved drippings
and gravy mix. Microwave at
High 2 to 6 minutes, or until
thickened, blending with wire
whip 2 or 3 times.

Texas Chili
After the Game, page 22

4 lbs. beef boneless chuck
  roast
1 large onion, chopped
1 medium green pepper,
  chopped
3 cloves garlic, minced
3 tablespoons olive oil
2 cans (28 oz. each) whole
  tomatoes, undrained

1 can (12 oz.) tomato paste
1 can (4 oz.) chopped green
  chilies, drained
4 to 6 teaspoons chili powder
1 tablespoon sugar
1½ teaspoons salt
¼ teaspoon pepper
2 cans (15 oz. each) kidney
  beans, drained

Serves 10 to 12

Trim excess fat from meat; discard. Cut meat into ½-in. cubes. In
5-qt. casserole combine cubes, onion, green pepper, garlic and
olive oil. Stir in remaining ingredients except kidney beans; cover.

Microwave at 70% (Medium-High) 5 minutes. Reduce power to
50% (Medium). Microwave 1¾ to 2 hours, or until meat is tender,
stirring several times. Mix in kidney beans. Let stand, covered, 10
to 15 minutes.

Advance preparation: Prepare the day before; cover and
refrigerate. To reheat, place in 5-qt. casserole. Microwave at 70%
(Medium-High) 45 to 60 minutes, or until heated, stirring once or
twice. Or place in two 2-qt. casseroles; cover. Microwave one at a
time at 70% (Medium-High) 15 to 30 minutes, or until heated,
stirring once or twice. Repeat with remaining casserole.

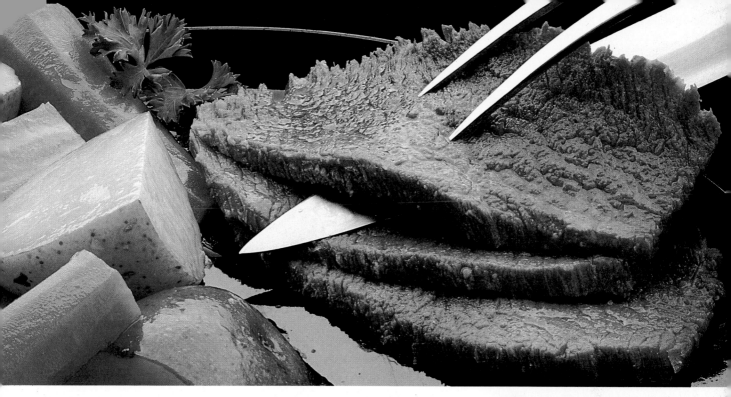

Corned Beef & ▲ Vegetables
Saint Patrick's Day, page 52

5 medium potatoes
6 medium carrots
5 lb. corned beef brisket with seasoning packet or 2 equalling 5 to 5½ lbs.
1 large onion, sliced
1 cup hot water

Serves 6 to 8

Cut potatoes into 1½- to 2-in. pieces. Cut carrots in half crosswise, then lengthwise into quarters. Set aside.

Place corned beef and one seasoning packet in 5-qt. casserole. Add onion and water; cover. Microwave at High 10 minutes. Reduce power to 50% (Medium). Microwave, covered, 45 minutes. Turn meat over. Add potatoes and carrots.

Microwave, covered, at 50% (Medium) 1 to 1½ hours, or until meat is fork tender. Let stand, 10 to 20 minutes. Remove meat and vegetables with slotted spoon; arrange on platter.

Sloppy Joes ▶
Halloween, page 64

2 medium onions, chopped
1 medium green pepper, chopped
1 tablespoon butter or margarine
2 lbs. ground beef
1 can (10¾ oz.) condensed tomato soup
½ cup chili sauce
⅓ cup packed brown sugar
1 tablespoon vinegar
1 tablespoon prepared mustard
1 can (6 oz.) tomato paste
1 teaspoon salt
¼ teaspoon black pepper
12 hamburger buns

Serves 12

Place onions, green pepper and butter in 3-qt. casserole. Microwave at High 5 minutes, or until onions are tender. Crumble ground beef into casserole. Microwave at High 8 to 13 minutes, or until meat is no longer pink, stirring 2 or 3 times during cooking. Drain.

Stir in remaining ingredients except buns; cover. Microwave at High 5 to 9 minutes, or until hot and bubbly, stirring after half the time. Serve in buns.

Manicotti ▶

Foreign Affair: Italian, page 40

16 manicotti shells

Filling:
1 lb. ground beef
1 pkg. (10 oz.) frozen
   chopped spinach,
   defrosted and drained
1 medium onion, chopped
3 eggs, beaten
1 cup fresh bread crumbs
3 tablespoons grated
   Parmesan cheese
½ teaspoon salt
¼ teaspoon pepper

Sauce:
2 cans (15 oz. each) tomato
   sauce
1 teaspoon sugar
¾ teaspoon dried oregano
   leaves
½ teaspoon dried basil leaves

Topping:
1 cup ricotta cheese
2 tablespoons grated
   Parmesan cheese
2 teaspoons fresh snipped
   parsley

Serves 8

Advance preparation: Prepare shells and filling. Fill shells and arrange in dishes. Place plastic wrap directly on shells. Refrigerate. Prepare sauce as directed. Cover and refrigerate. To serve, microwave sauce at High 2 to 3 minutes, or until hot. Pour sauce equally over shells in each dish. Cover with wax paper. Microwave each dish at High 8 minutes. Prepare topping and spoon over sauce. Reduce power to 70% (Medium-High). Microwave each dish 7 to 10 minutes, or until heated, rotating once or twice. Repeat with remaining dish.

How to Microwave Manicotti

Prepare manicotti shells as directed on package. Rinse in cold water; drain. Crumble ground beef into 3-qt. casserole; add onion. Microwave at High 4 to 6 minutes, or until beef is no longer pink; drain. Mix remaining filling ingredients with ground beef. Fill each shell. Arrange in single layer in two 12 × 8-in. baking dishes.

Mix all sauce ingredients. Pour equally over manicotti in both dishes. Combine topping ingredients. Spoon randomly over sauce. Microwave one dish at a time at High 5 to 8 minutes, or until sauce is bubbly and manicotti are heated, rotating dish once. Repeat with remaining dish.

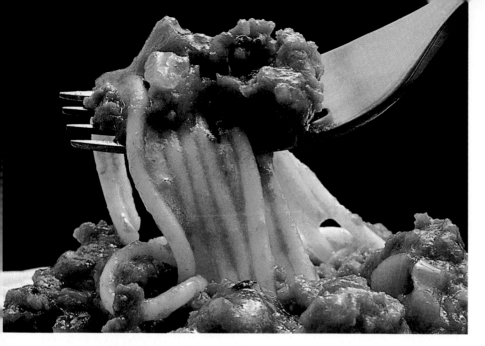

Italian Spaghetti Sauce ▲
Freezer Dinner, page 34

1 lb. ground beef
1 lb. bulk Italian sausage
2 medium onions, chopped
1 large green pepper,
    chopped
1 large clove garlic, minced
2 tablespoons olive oil
2 cans (15 oz. each) tomato
    sauce
1 can (16 oz.) whole tomatoes
2 cups hot water or 1 cup hot
    water plus 1 cup red wine

1 can (6 oz.) tomato paste
1 large bay leaf
2 teaspoons dried oregano
    leaves
1 teaspoon salt
1 teaspoon sugar
1 teaspoon dried parsley flakes
1 teaspoon dried basil leaves
½ teaspoon dried savory leaves
½ teaspoon dried marjoram
    leaves

Serves 2 to 12

In 2-qt. casserole crumble ground beef and sausage. Microwave at High 5 to 8 minutes, or until meat is no longer pink, stirring once or twice. Drain; set aside.

In 5-qt. casserole combine onions, green pepper, garlic and olive oil. Microwave, covered, at High 4 to 8 minutes, or until vegetables are tender. Stir in meat and remaining ingredients. Microwave, uncovered, at High 10 minutes. Reduce power to 70% (Medium-High). Microwave 45 minutes to 1½ hours, or until sauce is desired consistency and flavors are blended. Remove bay leaf. Place in freezer containers or plastic freezer bags in quantities of 2 or 4 servings. Each serving is about ¾ cup.

To serve, place frozen sauce in casserole and microwave, covered, at High as directed in chart, breaking up sauce with fork and stirring 2 or 3 times. If cover does not fit at first, break up sauce after first 5 minutes; cover. Serve over hot spaghetti, if desired.

Servings	Casserole Size	Microwave Time
2	1-qt.	6 to 9 minutes
4	1- to 1½-qt.	12 to 17 minutes
8	2- to 3-qt.	20 to 8 minutes
12	3- to 5-qt.	25 to 35 minutes

Barbecued Ribs
Labor Day, page 62

7½ to 9 lbs. pork spareribs, cut
    into 2- or 3-rib pieces
¾ cup water, divided
    Barbecue Sauce, below

Serves 10 to 12

Arrange one-third of ribs at a time in single layer in 12 × 8-in. baking dish or 3-qt. casserole, overlapping slightly as needed. Add ¼ cup water; cover tightly with plastic wrap. Microwave at High 5 minutes. Reduce power to 50% (Medium). Microwave, covered, 15 to 20 minutes, turning ribs over once. Drain. Repeat twice with remaining ribs. Place on grill over hot charcoal. Cook until fork tender, basting with barbecue sauce.

Barbecue Sauce

1½ cups chopped onion
1½ teaspoons minced garlic
1 tablespoon vegetable oil
⅓ cup packed dark brown
    sugar
1½ teaspoons dried basil
    leaves
1½ teaspoons salt
¼ teaspoon pepper
3 cans (28 oz. each) whole
    tomatoes, drained
⅓ cup catsup
¼ cup plus 2 teaspoons cider
    vinegar
2 tablespoons dark molasses
2 tablespoons Worcestershire
    sauce
1 tablespoon prepared
    mustard
2 teaspoons liquid smoke
¼ to ½ teaspoon red pepper
    sauce

Makes 2 to 2½ cups

In 3-qt. casserole combine onion, garlic and oil; cover. Microwave at High 3 to 5 minutes, or until tender. Mix in remaining ingredients. Microwave at High 50 to 60 minutes, or until tomatoes are soft and liquid is absorbed. Push through metal strainer to pureé tomatoes and remove seeds.

Crown Roast of Pork

Dinner Party for Eight, page 16

Stuffing:

1½ to 2 lbs. ground pork
2 stalks celery, thinly sliced
1 medium onion, chopped
¼ cup butter or margarine
2 cups fresh white bread
  cubes
2 cups fresh rye bread cubes
⅓ cup chopped spiced
  peaches
¼ cup raisins

3 tablespoons snipped fresh
  parsley
¾ teaspoon poultry seasoning
½ teaspoon salt
⅛ teaspoon pepper

Roast:

1 teaspoon dried marjoram
1 teaspoon seasoned salt
½ teaspoon poultry seasoning
6 to 7-lb. crown roast of pork

Serves 8

Advance preparation: Prepare stuffing the day before; cover and refrigerate. Roast will keep warm, covered, an additional 20 minutes after standing time.

Total Cooking Time:
15 to 17 min./lb.

How to Microwave Crown Roast of Pork

Microwave ground pork in 3-qt. casserole or large bowl at High 5 to 9 minutes, or until meat is no longer pink, stirring once or twice. Drain. Set aside.

Combine celery, onion and butter in 1-qt. casserole. Microwave at High 3 to 5 minutes, or until tender. Stir remaining stuffing ingredients into ground pork; cover. Set aside. Combine roast seasonings in small dish.

Rub seasoning mixture into pork roast. Place roast bone ends down on roasting rack. Estimate total cooking time and divide in half. Microwave at High 5 minutes. Reduce power to 50% (Medium). Microwave remainder of first half of time.

Turn roast over. Fill cavity lightly with stuffing. Cover stuffing with plastic wrap to keep moist. Microwave remaining time or until internal temperature reaches 165°F.

Tent loosely with foil. Let stand 10 minutes, or until internal temperature reaches 170°F, when checked in several places.

Remove roast to serving platter, using spatula to support stuffing. Decorate ends with paper frills or additional spiced peaches, if desired. Carve down between chops to serve.

Fruited Pork Roast ▶

Christmas Eve, page 72

¾ cup packed brown sugar,
   divided
¾ cup dried apricot halves,
   halved
½ cup dried prunes, halved
   and pitted
¾ cup hot water
¼ cup plus 2 tablespoons
   frozen orange juice concentrate, defrosted and divided
1 small onion, sliced
½ teaspoon ground ginger
¼ teaspoon salt
⅛ teaspoon pepper
1 tablespoon butter or margarine
3 lb. boneless pork loin roast

Serves 6 to 8

In 1-qt. casserole combine ½
cup brown sugar, the apricots,
prunes, water, ¼ cup orange
concentrate, the onion, ginger,
salt and pepper. Microwave at
High 8 to 12 minutes, or until
fruit is softened, stirring every 4
minutes. Set aside.

Melt butter in small bowl at High
30 to 45 seconds. Stir in
remaining ¼ cup brown sugar
and 2 tablespoons concentrate.

Place roast fat side down on
roasting rack. Spread with
butter mixture. Estimate total
cooking time; divide in half.
Microwave at High 5 minutes.
Reduce power to 50%
(Medium). Microwave remaining
part of first half of time.

Turn roast over. Insert meat
thermometer. Spoon half of
sauce over top. Microwave at
50% (Medium) for second half
of time, or until internal
temperature reaches 165°F.
Spoon on remaining sauce. Let
stand, tented loosely with foil,
10 minutes, or until internal
temperature reaches 170°F.,
checking in several places.

Total Cooking Time:
12 to 18 min./lb.

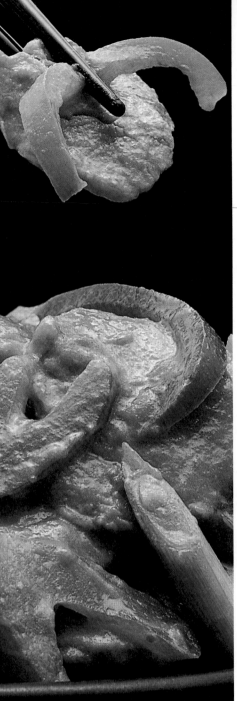

Red-Glazed Pork
Foreign Affair: Oriental, page 38

3 tablespoons butter or
  margarine
1½ lbs. pork tenderloin, thinly
  sliced
1 cup thin diagonal slices
  celery
1 small green pepper, cut into
  ¼-in. strips
¾ cup green onion slices, ½-in.
⅓ cup soy sauce
2 tablespoons cornstarch
3 tablespoons tomato paste
2 tablespoons vinegar

Serves 6 to 8

Melt butter in 2-qt. casserole at
High 45 to 60 seconds. Stir in
pork, celery and green pepper
until coated. Cover. Microwave
at High 5 to 9 minutes, or just
until pork is no longer pink,
stirring 2 or 3 times. Stir in
green onion; cover. Set aside.

In small bowl blend soy sauce,
cornstarch, tomato paste and
vinegar. Microwave at High 1 to
3½ minutes, or until thickened,
stirring with wire whip 2 or 3
times. Slowly stir mixture into
casserole. Microwave at High 1
to 2 minutes, or until heated.

Advance preparation: Pork
and vegetables can be sliced
the night before or early in the
day. Microwave up to 30
minutes in advance; let stand,
covered. Reheat, covered, at
High 3 to 5 minutes.

Apricot-Glazed Ham
Christmas Day, page 74

3 lb. fully cooked boneless ham 1 jar (10 oz.) apricot preserves

Serves 6 to 8

Place ham fat side down on roasting rack or 8 × 8-in. baking dish.
Cover cut surface with plastic wrap. Microwave at 50% (Medium)
20 minutes. Turn ham over.

Score ham fat in 1-in. diamonds, cutting only ¼ inch deep.
Microwave at 50% (Medium) 10 minutes. Spread three-fourths of
preserves over ham. Microwave at 50% (Medium) 10 to 15
minutes, or until internal temperature reaches 130°F. Top with
remaining preserves. Let stand, tented with foil, 5 to 10 minutes.

Glazed Ham
New Year's Day, page 48

½ cup packed brown sugar
2 tablespoons prepared mustard
5 lb. fully cooked boneless ham

Serves 20

In small bowl mix brown sugar
and mustard. Score ham fat in
diamonds, cutting only ¼ inch
deep. Place ham scored side
up in 8 × 8-in. baking dish.
Spread glaze over ham.
Microwave at High 10 to 15
minutes, or until glaze is set,
basting twice. Serve ham cold.

Advance preparation: Prepare
the day before. Cover and
refrigerate. To serve, microwave
at High 5 to 10 minutes, or until
glaze is reheated.

Creamy Veal
Valentine's Day, page 50

2 tablespoons butter or
  margarine
1 tablespoon plus 1½
  teaspoons all-purpose flour
½ teaspoon salt
¼ teaspoon pepper
¾ lb. boneless veal loin, cut into
  ¾-in. cubes
⅓ cup half and half or milk
2 tablespoons white wine
2 teaspoons snipped fresh
  parsley

Serves 2

Melt butter in 1-qt. casserole at
High 30 to 45 seconds. Set
aside. In plastic bag combine
flour, salt and pepper. Add
meat; shake until coated. Stir
meat and remaining flour into
butter. Mix in half and half, wine
and parsley; cover.

Reduce power to 50%
(Medium). Microwave 5 to 12
minutes, or until meat is fork
tender and sauce is thickened,
stirring once. Serve over hot
cooked fettuccine, if desired.

Advance preparation: Prepare
the day before. Cover and
refrigerate. Microwave at 50%
(Medium) 4 to 9 minutes, or
until hot, stirring once.

Lamb Meatballs

Foreign Affair: East Indian, page 42

1½ lbs. ground lamb
¼ cup fresh snipped mint or 2 tablespoons dried mint flakes
1 teaspoon salt, divided
⅛ teaspoon pepper
2 tablespoons butter or margarine
1 large onion, chopped
1 clove garlic, minced
½ cup hot water
¼ cup raisins, optional
1 teaspoon instant chicken bouillon granules
1 teaspoon all-purpose flour
1 teaspoon turmeric
1 teaspoon ground ginger
½ teaspoon chili powder

Serves 6 to 8

Mix ground lamb, mint, ½ teaspoon salt and the pepper. Shape by tablespoonfuls into meatballs. Place in 12 × 8-in. baking dish. Microwave at High 4 to 7 minutes, or until meatballs are firm and no longer pink, stirring 2 or 3 times during cooking. Drain and set aside.

In 1½-qt. casserole, combine butter, onion and garlic. Microwave at High, 3½ to 5½ minutes, or until onion is tender. Blend in ½ teaspoon salt and remaining ingredients except meatballs. Microwave at High 1 to 3 minutes, or until sauce is bubbly. Stir to blend. Stir in meatballs until coated. Micro-wave at High, 1 to 3 minutes, or until meatballs are heated.

Advance preparation: Prepare meatballs the day before. Drain; cover and refrigerate. At serving time, prepare sauce. Stir in meatballs; cover. Microwave at High 3 to 7 minutes, or until meatballs are heated, stirring once or twice during cooking.

Lamb Roast ▼

Easter, page 54

4 lb. boneless rolled leg of lamb roast
2 cloves garlic, cut in thin slices
½ teaspoon dried thyme leaves
½ teaspoon dried rosemary leaves
½ teaspoon dried chervil leaves
½ teaspoon onion salt
¼ teaspoon pepper

Serves 8

Cut small slits in lamb roast. Insert garlic slices in slits. Combine remaining ingredients; rub over roast. Place roast, fat side down, on baking rack. Estimate total cooking time from chart, below; divide in half. Microwave at High 5 minutes. Reduce power to 50% (Medium). Microwave remaining part of first half of cooking time.

Turn roast over. Insert meat thermometer or probe. Microwave at 50% (Medium) for last half of cooking time, or until internal temperature reaches removal point for desired doneness. Let stand, tented with foil, 10 minutes.

Desired Doneness	Min./lb.	Removal Temp.
Rare	8½ to 12½	120°F.
Medium	10 to 14¼	135°F.
Well	11½ to 16	150°F.

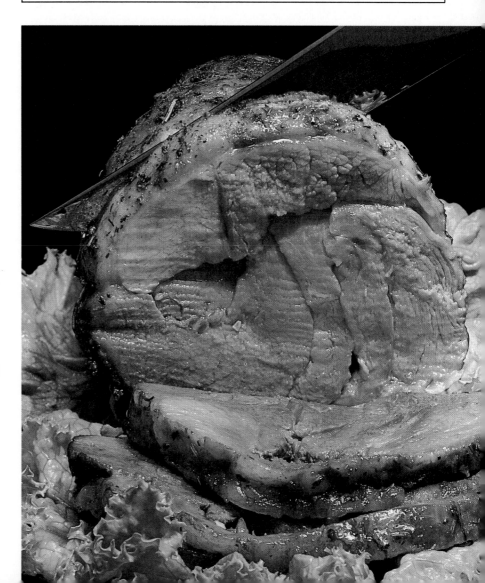

Chicken With Sherried Cheese Sauce

Adult Birthday Party, page 24

¼ cup plus 2 tablespoons butter or margarine, divided
1 cup bread crumbs
2 tablespoons grated Parmesan cheese
1 tablespoon dried parsley flakes
1 teaspoon paprika
4 large whole boneless chicken breasts, split and skin removed
2 tablespoons all-purpose flour
½ teaspoon salt
Dash pepper
1¼ cups milk
2 tablespoons sherry
1 cup shredded Swiss cheese
Dash nutmeg

Serves 8

Place ¼ cup butter in 9-in. pie plate. Microwave at High 45 to 60 seconds, or until melted. In another pie plate mix bread crumbs, Parmesan cheese, parsley and paprika. Dip each chicken piece in butter, then coat with crumb mixture. Place on baking sheet. Microwave at High 10 to 14 minutes, or until no longer pink, rearranging after half the time but do not turn over. Let stand, covered.

Place 2 tablespoons butter in 4-cup measure. Microwave at High 30 to 45 seconds, or until melted. Stir in flour, salt and pepper. Blend in milk and sherry. Microwave at High 4 to 5 minutes, or until thickened. Blend in Swiss cheese and nutmeg until cheese melts. Serve over chicken. Garnish with almonds and sliced black olives, if desired.

Turkey

Thanksgiving, page 66

11 lb. ready-to-cook turkey, giblets removed

Serves 12 to 14

Place turkey, breast side down, in baking dish. Microwave at High 10 minutes. Reduce power to 50% (Medium). Microwave 27 minutes, checking occasionally and shielding with foil as needed. Turn turkey on its side. Microwave at 50% (Medium) 37 minutes. (Baste and shield turkey as needed.)

Turn turkey on its other side. Microwave 37 minutes. Turn turkey breast side up. Shield with foil as needed. Microwave at 50% (Medium) 21 to 54 minutes or until legs move freely and juices run clear, basting as needed. Check internal temperature in several places. It should register 170°F. Let stand, tented with foil, at least 20 minutes.

Advance preparation: Turkey can stand up to 45 minutes before carving.

Turkey Breast

Freezer Buffet, page 36

4 to 5-lb. turkey breast

Serves 10 to 12

Place turkey breast skin side down in 12 × 8-in. baking dish. Estimate the total cooking time; divide in half. Microwave at High first 5 minutes. Reduce power to 50% (Medium). Microwave remaining part of first half of time. Turn skin side up. Glaze with jelly if desired.

Microwave remaining time, or until internal temperature of meatiest area is 170°F. Let stand 10 to 20 minutes, tented with foil.

> Total Cooking Time:
> 10½ to 15 min./lb.

Advance preparation: Prepare turkey breast the day before serving. Cut into thin slices; cover and refrigerate. To serve, microwave plate of sliced turkey, covered, at High 1 to 4 minutes, or until chill is removed.

Spanish Chicken ▲

Foreign Affair: Spanish, page 44

1 jar (10 oz.) pimiento-stuffed green olives, drained
8 oz. fresh mushrooms, sliced
4 whole boneless chicken breasts, split and skin removed
2 slices bacon, cut up
1 tablespoon all-purpose flour
¾ cup red wine
½ teaspoon salt

Serves 6 to 8

In 12 × 8-in. baking dish layer olives, mushrooms and chicken breasts. Set aside. Place bacon in 2-cup measure. Microwave at High 1½ to 3 minutes, or until crisp. Remove bacon with slotted spoon. Blend flour into bacon drippings. Stir in wine and salt. Microwave at High 1 to 3 minutes, or until thickened. Add bacon. Pour over chicken. Cover with wax paper.

Microwave at High 8 to 11 minutes, or until chicken is no longer pink, rearranging chicken once. Let stand 5 minutes.

Five Boy Chicken Curry

Foreign Affair: East Indian, page 42

2 tablespoons butter or
    margarine
1 cup chopped onion
½ cup chopped celery
2 cloves garlic, minced
⅓ cup all-purpose flour
½ teaspoon dried thyme leaves
½ teaspoon salt
¼ teaspoon pepper
5 to 6 lbs. broiler-fryer
    chicken pieces
2 tablespoons curry powder
1 can (16 oz.) whole tomatoes
1 cup whipping cream

Condiments:

Almonds
Toasted coconut
Crumbled crisp bacon
Watermelon pickles
Chopped hard cooked
    eggs

Serves 6 to 8

In 5-qt. casserole combine butter, onion, celery and garlic. Microwave at High 2 to 4 minutes, or until onion is tender. In plastic bag combine flour, thyme, salt and pepper. Shake chicken in bag to coat. Blend curry powder into butter mixture. Add chicken, remaining flour mixture and tomatoes; cover.

Microwave at High 28 to 38 minutes, or until chicken is tender and meat near bone is no longer pink, stirring 3 or 4 times. Arrange chicken on serving platter. Stir cream into cooking liquid. Serve sauce and condiments separately.

Advance preparation: Prepare the day before but do not add cream. When reheating, microwave at High 20 to 28 minutes, rearranging after half the time, or until chicken is heated. Remove chicken, stir in whipping cream.

Chicken Roulades ▲

Freezer Dinner, page 30

1 cup chopped mushrooms
¼ cup chopped onion
¼ cup chopped celery
1 small clove garlic, minced
1 tablespoon olive oil or butter
2 tablespoons seasoned
    bread crumbs
¼ teaspoon salt
Dash pepper
2 whole boneless chicken
    breasts, skin removed
¼ cup seasoned bread crumbs
½ teaspoon dried parsley flakes
Mushroom Sauce, below

Serves 2

In 1-qt. casserole combine mushrooms, onion, celery, garlic and oil. Microwave at High 2 to 4 minutes, or until tender. Stir in 2 tablespoons bread crumbs, the salt and pepper.

Place chicken breasts between wax paper. Pound to flatten to ¼-in. thickness. Spread half of stuffing mixture in center of each. Fold sides of chicken over stuffing; secure with wooden pick. Mix ¼ cup bread crumbs and the parsley flakes. Roll chicken in mixture to coat. Wrap securely; label and freeze up to 1 month.

To serve, place frozen breasts in 8 × 8-in. baking dish. Cover with wax paper. Microwave at High 5 minutes. Reduce power to 50% (Medium). Microwave 9 to 14 minutes, or until chicken is no longer pink, rearranging once. Serve with Mushroom Sauce.

Mushroom Sauce

2 cups sliced mushrooms
¼ cup chopped onion
1 tablespoon plus 1½ tea-
    spoons butter or margarine
1 tablespoon plus 1½
    teaspoons all-purpose flour
¼ teaspoon salt
⅛ teaspoon pepper
½ cup whipping cream
¼ cup white wine

Makes about 1½ cups

In 1-qt. casserole combine mushrooms, onion and butter. Microwave at High 2 to 3 minutes, or until tender. Stir in flour, salt and pepper. Blend in cream. Microwave at High 2 to 3½ minutes, or until thickened and bubbly, stirring once or twice. Mix in wine. Microwave at High 30 seconds, or until heated.

◄ Chicken & Pea Pods
Foreign Affair: Oriental, page 38

Chicken & Pea Pods

1 tablespoon cornstarch
¼ cup soy sauce
2 teaspoons fresh grated
 gingerroot*
2½ lbs. boneless chicken
 breasts, skin removed, cut
 into strips
2 pkgs. (6 oz. each) frozen
 pea pods
¾ cup cashews or almonds

Serves 6 to 8

In 1½- to 2-qt. casserole combine cornstarch, soy sauce and gingerroot. Microwave at High 1½ minutes. Add chicken. Cover. Microwave at High 4 minutes.

Stir in pea pods. Microwave, covered, at High 5½ to 11 minutes, or until chicken is no longer pink and pea pods are tender-crisp, stirring once or twice to break up pea pods. Stir in cashews. Serve with additional soy sauce, if desired.

*Wrap the unpeeled gingerroot tightly in foil and freeze. To use, remove a bit of the peel and shave the frozen gingerroot with a knife rather than grating it.

Advance preparation: Chicken can be cut into strips early in the day; cover and refrigerate. Chicken & Pea Pods can stand, covered, up to 20 minutes before serving. Reheat at High 1 to 2 minutes, if needed.

Cold Fried Chicken
Fourth of July, page 60

2 envelopes (4¼ oz. each)
 crispy crumb coating for
 chicken
1½ cups crushed whole wheat
 flake cereal
2 tablespoons dried parsley
 flakes

1 teaspoon salt
½ cup butter or margarine
2 eggs
3 tablespoons milk
8 to 9 lbs. broiler-fryer
 chicken pieces

Serves 12

In shallow dish mix crumb coating, cereal, parsley flakes and salt. Set aside. Place butter in pie plate. Microwave at High 45 seconds to 1¼ minutes, or until melted. Beat in eggs and milk. Dip chicken pieces in egg mixture, then dredge in crumb-cereal mixture, pressing firmly to coat.

Place one-third of pieces bone side down on paper towel-lined baking sheet with meatiest parts towards outside. Microwave at High 12 minutes. Rearrange so less cooked parts are towards outside; do not turn over. Microwave at High 10 to 15 minutes, or until juices run clear and meat near bone is no longer pink. Repeat with remaining chicken. Refrigerate, uncovered, until cool. Wrap or pack in container.

Advance preparation: Prepare the day before; refrigerate.

Barbecued Chicken
Labor Day, page 62

7½ to 10½ lbs. broiler-fryer
 chicken pieces
 Barbecue Sauce, page 95

Serves 10 to 12

Arrange 2½ to 3½ lbs. chicken pieces on roasting rack or in 12 × 8-in. baking dish. Microwave at High 4 minutes/lb., rearranging once. Repeat until all chicken is microwaved.

Place on grill over hot charcoal; cook until fork tender, basting with barbecue sauce. Repeat with remaining chicken.

Chicken & Rice

New Year's Eve, page 46

3½ lbs. boneless chicken
   breasts
½ cup white wine
   Hot water
2 cups uncooked long grain
   rice
½ cup chopped green onion
2 tablespoons instant chicken
   bouillon granules
½ teaspoon pepper
1 cup coarsely chopped
   roasted peanuts

Serves 6 to 8

In 12 × 8-in. baking dish combine chicken breasts and white wine; cover. Microwave at High 10 to 18 minutes, or until chicken is no longer pink, rearranging once or twice during cooking. Remove skin; discard. Cut chicken into bite-size pieces. Set aside. Drain cooking liquid into 4-cup measure. Add hot water to equal 3½ cups.

In 3-qt. casserole combine cooking liquid, rice, green onion, instant bouillon and pepper; cover. Microwave at High 8 minutes. Reduce power to (50%) Medium. Microwave 25 to 30 minutes, or until rice is tender and liquid is absorbed. Add chicken and peanuts. Let stand, covered, 10 minutes.

Advance preparation: Prepare chicken the day before. Discard skin; reserve liquid. Cover and refrigerate chicken and liquid separately. To reheat, let chicken stand at room temperature while preparing rice. Microwave cooking liquid plus hot water at High 2 to 4 minutes, or until heated; stir in rice, instant bouillon and pepper. Continue as directed above. When rice is tender, microwave chicken at High 1 to 4 minutes, or until heated. Add to rice with peanuts. Let stand, covered, 10 minutes.

Hot Chicken Salad ►

Spring Open House, page 20

2 large onions, chopped
2 green peppers, chopped
½ cup butter or margarine
8 cups cut-up, cooked
   chicken, ½-in. cubes*
1½ cups sliced almonds
¾ cup unseasoned bread
   cubes
1 tablespoon plus 1 teaspoon
   instant chicken
   bouillon granules
1 teaspoon salt
½ teaspoon pepper
½ cup brandy
¼ cup water
⅛ to ¼ teaspoon red pepper
   sauce
5 cups shredded lettuce
1½ cups halved seedless green
   grapes

Serves 20

Place onion, green pepper and butter in 5-qt. casserole. Microwave at High 4 to 7 minutes, or until vegetables are tender-crisp. Stir in remaining ingredients except lettuce and grapes. Microwave at High 6 to 13 minutes, or until heated, stirring once. Mix in lettuce and grapes.

*A 3-lb. cooked boneless turkey breast, cut into ½-in. cubes can be used. Or use four 2½-lb. cooked broiler-fryer chickens, boned and cut into ½-in. cubes.

Advance preparation: Chicken or turkey can be cooked and cubed the day before. Cover and refrigerate. Early in day combine all ingredients except lettuce and grapes. Cover and refrigerate. To serve, microwave, covered, at High 10 to 15 minutes, or until heated, stirring once or twice.

Wine-Poached Fish

Simple Dinner for Four, page 14

1 lb. fresh fish fillets
¼ cup white wine
½ teaspoon salt
¼ teaspoon pepper
1 tomato, thinly sliced
2 teaspoons fresh snipped
   parsley
¼ teaspoon dried basil leaves
1 tablespoon butter or
   margarine

Serves 4

In 12 × 8 in. baking dish place fish fillets in single layer with thickest portions to outside of dish. Add wine. Sprinkle fillets with salt and pepper. Top with tomato slices. Sprinkle with parsley and basil; dot with butter. Cover with plastic wrap.

Microwave at High 4 to 7 minutes, or until fish flakes easily with fork, rotating once or twice. Let stand, covered, 5 to 10 minutes.

Eggs & Cheese

◄ Double Cheese Quiche
Midnight Supper, page 26

2 tablespoons dry bread
    crumbs
½ cup shredded Swiss
    cheese
½ cup shredded Cheddar
    cheese.
2 tablespoons finely chopped
    onion
2 tablespoons finely chopped
    green pepper
¼ cup buttermilk baking mix
¾ teaspoon salt
⅛ teaspoon pepper
5 eggs
1⅓ cups half and half

Serves 6

Butter bottom of 8- or 9-in.
quiche dish. Coat with crumbs.
Sprinkle Swiss and Cheddar
cheese in dish. In 2-qt.
casserole combine onion and
green pepper. Microwave at
High 2 to 4 minutes, or until
tender, stirring 2 or 3 times. Stir
in baking mix, salt and pepper
until vegetables are coated.
Beat in eggs and half and half.

Reduce power to 50%
(Medium). Microwave 5 to 8
minutes, or until very hot but not
set, stirring with wire whip every
2 minutes. Stir; pour into dish.
Microwave at 50% (Medium) 8
to 12 minutes, or until knife
inserted halfway between center
and edge comes out clean and
quiche is almost set, rotating
dish ¼ turn every 3 to 4
minutes. Let stand 10 minutes
before cutting.

Advance preparation: Cover
and refrigerate microwaved
quiche no longer than 8 hours
or overnight. Microwave at 50%
(Medium) 10 to 15 minutes, or
until heated.

Egg & Sausage Bake ▲
Mother's Day, page 56

1 pkg. (12 oz.) seasoned bulk
   pork sausage
¼ cup chopped green pepper
¼ cup chopped onion
8 eggs
½ cup milk
¼ teaspoon salt
⅛ teaspoon pepper
1 cup shredded Cheddar
   cheese
1 cup shredded Swiss cheese

Serves 4

Crumble sausage into 2-qt. casserole. Add green pepper and onion. Microwave at High 3 to 6 minutes, or until meat is no longer pink, stirring to break apart after half the time. Break sausage into small pieces; drain well. Spread in 8 × 8-in. baking dish. Set aside.

Beat eggs, milk, salt and pepper in 2-qt. casserole. Reduce power to 50% (Medium). Microwave 5 to 9 minutes, or until eggs are set but still very moist, stirring every 2 minutes. Stir in cheeses; pour over sausage. Cover with wax paper.

Place on inverted saucer in oven. Microwave at 50% (Medium) 10 to 12 minutes, or until center is set, but slightly moist on top, rotating ¼ turn every 3 minutes. Let stand, covered, 5 minutes.

Party Quiche
Cocktail Party Buffet, page 18

Crust:
⅓ cup shortening
1 tablespoon butter or
   margarine
1¼ cups all-purpose flour
½ teaspoon salt
2 to 3 tablespoons cold water
   with 2 drops yellow food
   coloring
1 egg, separated
½ teaspoon water

Filling:
10 slices bacon, chopped
4 eggs
1 can (13 oz.) evaporated
   milk
½ teaspoon salt
⅛ teaspoon cayenne
1 cup shredded Swiss
   cheese
⅓ cup chopped green onion

Serves 8

Cut shortening and butter into flour and salt until particles resemble small peas. Sprinkle with water mixture, 1 tablespoon at a time, stirring with fork until dough forms a ball. Roll out to 12-in. square on floured surface. Gently place in 10-in. square casserole. Crimp edges so dough covers ¾ to 1 inch up sides of casserole. Prick with fork. Microwave at High 3 to 6 minutes, or until crust is dry.

Combine egg yolk and ½ teaspoon water. Brush crust with yolk mixture. Microwave at High 30 to 60 seconds, or until yolk is set. Set crust aside.

In 2-qt. casserole microwave bacon at High 6 to 9 minutes, or until crisp, stirring 2 or 3 times. Remove bacon to paper towel with slotted spoon. Discard fat. .

In the same casserole combine reserved egg white and the 4 eggs, evaporated milk, salt and cayenne. Blend thoroughly. Reduce power to 50% (Medium). Microwave 4 to 6 minutes, or until very hot but not set, stirring with wire whip every 1 to 2 minutes during cooking time.

Layer cheese, bacon and green onion in crust. Pour in egg mixture. Cover with wax paper. Place in oven on inverted pie plate or dinner plate. Reduce power to 30% (Medium-Low). Microwave 20 to 28 minutes, or until just set, rotating 3 or 4 times during cooking time. Let stand 10 minutes.

Advance preparation: Prepare the day before or early in the day; refrigerate. To serve, cut into 16 pieces and place on platter. Cover with wax paper. Microwave at 50% (Medium) 3 to 6 minutes, or until heated, rearranging pieces once.

Vegetables

◀ Asparagus Spears

Freezer Dinner, page 30

1 pkg. (8 oz.) frozen
   asparagus spears
2 tablespoons hot water
2 tablespoons butter or
   margarine
1 tablespoon white wine
¼ cup sunflower nuts

Serves 2

Place asparagus and water in
1-qt. casserole; cover.
Microwave at High 4 to 7
minutes, or until asparagus is
tender and hot, breaking up
once. Let stand, covered, 3 to
5 minutes.

Place butter in small bowl.
Microwave at High 30 to 45
seconds, or until melted. Blend
in wine. Pour sauce over
asparagus and top with
sunflower nuts.

Lemony Asparagus

Easter, page 54

2 lbs. fresh asparagus spears
¼ cup hot water
½ cup butter or margarine
2 tablespoons lemon juice
2 hard cooked eggs, finely
   chopped

Serves 8

Snap off tough ends of
asparagus. Place spears in
12 × 8-in. baking dish. Add
water; cover. Microwave at High
4 to 8½ minutes, or until tender,
rearranging spears and rotating
dish after half the time. Let
stand 5 minutes; drain.

Place butter and lemon juice in
small bowl. Microwave at High
1 to 1½ minutes, or until butter
is melted. Stir. Pour over
asparagus spears; sprinkle with
chopped eggs.

Baked Beans

Labor Day, page 62

1 pkg. (16 oz.) dried Northern
   beans
8 cups hot water
2 teaspoons salt, divided
¼ teaspoon pepper
8 slices bacon, cut into ½-in.
   pieces
2 cups chopped onion
⅓ cup dark molasses
1 can (6 oz.) tomato paste
2 tablespoons packed brown
   sugar
2 teaspoons prepared mustard

Serves 10 to 12

In 5-qt. casserole combine
beans, water, 1½ teaspoons
salt and the pepper. Cover and
let stand overnight. (Or,
microwave at High 10 to 14
minutes, or until water starts to
boil. Boil 2 minutes. Let stand,
covered 1 hour.) Add bacon
and onion; cover. Microwave at
High 40 to 50 minutes, or until
beans are tender, stirring
several times.

Drain all but 1½ cups liquid. Stir
in remaining ½ teaspoon salt,
the molasses, tomato paste,
brown sugar and mustard;
cover. Microwave at High 25 to
35 minutes, or until mixture is
thickened and beans have
absorbed flavors, stirring
several times during cooking.

Advance preparation: Can
stand 1 hour, covered, without
needing to be reheated. Or,
prepare the day before and
refrigerate. Microwave at High,
covered, 18 to 25 minutes, or
until hot, stirring 3 or 4 times.

◄ Sweet & Sour Green Beans
Adult Birthday Party, page 24

3 slices bacon, cut up
1 small onion, sliced and
    separated into rings
2 tablespoons packed brown
    sugar
½ teaspoon salt
¼ teaspoon dry mustard
2 tablespoons vinegar
1 pkg. (16 oz.) frozen
    French-style green beans

Serves 8

Place bacon and onion in small bowl. Microwave at High 2 to 3 minutes, or until onion is tender and bacon cooked, stirring once. Mix in brown sugar, salt, mustard and vinegar.

Place green beans in 2-qt. casserole. Cover with plastic wrap. Microwave at High 6 to 8 minutes, or until heated, stirring after half the time. Drain. Add bacon-onion mixture, tossing to combine. Microwave at High 2 to 3 minutes, or until heated.

Green Beans & Broccoli
Christmas Day, page 74

2 pkgs. (10 oz. each) frozen
    broccoli cuts
1 pkg. (10 oz.) frozen
    French-style green beans
¼ cup butter or margarine
½ teaspoon salt
⅛ teaspoon pepper

Serves 6 to 8

Place vegetables in 2-qt. casserole; cover. Microwave at High 9 to 15 minutes, or until heated and tender, stirring 2 or 3 times to break apart. Drain.

Place butter in small bowl. Microwave at High 45 to 60 seconds, or until melted. Add salt and pepper. Pour over vegetables, tossing to coat.

Advance preparation:
Vegetables can stand, covered, 15 minutes before serving.

Green Bean Casserole
Thanksgiving, page 66

5 tablespoons butter or
    margarine, divided
½ cup slivered almonds
3 pkgs. (9 oz. each) frozen
    French-style green beans
½ cup chopped onion

¼ cup all-purpose flour
2 teaspoons instant chicken
    bouillon granules
¾ teaspoon salt
¼ teaspoon white pepper
2½ cups half and half

Serves 12 to 14

Place 1 tablespoon butter in pie plate. Microwave at High 30 to 45 seconds, or until melted. Stir in almonds. Microwave at High 6 to 8 minutes, or until light brown, stirring once or twice. Let stand 5 minutes. Drain on paper towels.

Place green beans in 3-qt. casserole; cover. Microwave at High 13 to 15 minutes, or until tender, stirring after half the time to break apart beans.

Place 4 tablespoons butter and the onion in 2-qt. casserole. Microwave at High 1½ to 2 minutes. Stir in flour, bouillon granules, salt and pepper. Blend in half and half. Microwave at High 7 to 9 minutes, or until thickened, stirring after 2 minutes and then every minute. Drain green beans. Pour sauce over beans. Sprinkle with slivered almonds.

Lemony Broccoli ▶
Simple Dinner for Four, page 14

1½ lbs. fresh broccoli
½ cup hot water
⅓ cup butter or margarine
1 tablespoon fresh lemon
   juice
½ teaspoon salt

Serves 4

Trim 1 inch from stem end of broccoli. Cut broccoli into spears. Place in 12 × 8-in. baking dish with flowerets toward center. Add water; cover. Microwave at High 8 to 12½ minutes, or until fork tender, rotating dish once. Let stand 3 to 5 minutes; drain.

Microwave butter in small dish at High 45 seconds to 1¼ minutes, or until melted. Stir in lemon juice and salt. Pour over broccoli. Garnish with lemon twists, if desired.

Lemon-Buttered Brussels Sprouts
New Year's Day, page 48

4 pkgs. (16 oz. each) frozen
   Brussels sprouts
½ cup hot water
½ cup butter or margarine
1 tablespoon grated lemon
   peel
1 tablespoon lemon juice
½ teaspoon salt
   Dash pepper

Serves 20

In 5-qt. casserole combine Brussels sprouts and water; cover. Microwave at High 28 to 32 minutes, or until fork tender, stirring after half the cooking time. Set aside, covered

Place butter in small dish. Microwave at High 45 seconds to 1¼ minutes, or until melted. Stir in lemon peel, lemon juice, salt and pepper. Drain Brussels sprouts. Add lemon butter, tossing to coat.

Broccoli & Mushrooms ▼
New Year's Eve, page 46

1 lb. fresh broccoli flowerets
¼ cup hot water
1 lb. fresh mushrooms

2 cups Italian dressing or 1
   bottle (16 oz.) Italian dressing

Serves 6 to 8

In 3-qt. casserole combine broccoli and water; cover. Microwave at High 1 minute. Drain and rinse in cold water. In bowl or plastic bag combine broccoli, mushrooms and dressing. Refrigerate at least 8 hours. If using bowl, stir several times. Remove vegetables to serving platter with slotted spoon. Serve with cocktail picks.

Sunny Carrots
Freezer Impromptu Dinner, page 28

1½ cups frozen whole baby
    carrots
  2 teaspoons instant orange
    breakfast drink mix,
    divided

Serves 2

Place carrots in 1-qt. casserole.
Sprinkle with 1 teaspoon drink
mix; cover. Microwave at High 5
to 7 minutes, or until carrots are
fork tender. Drain. Sprinkle with
remaining 1 teaspoon drink mix.
Stir to coat. Let stand, covered,
5 minutes.

Carrot Noodles
Father's Day, page 58

  5 large carrots, peeled
¼ cup water
¼ cup butter or margarine
½ teaspoon sugar
½ teaspoon salt

Serves 4 to 6

Shave carrots into thin slices
the length of carrot using a
vegetable peeler.

In 2-qt. casserole combine all
ingredients; cover. Microwave at
High 6 to 8 minutes, or until
carrots are tender, stirring once
during cooking. Toss with fork
before serving.

Advance preparation: Carrots
can be peeled and shaved early
in the day. Place in cold water.
Let stand at room temperature.

Minted Carrots & ▲
Brussels Sprouts
Christmas Eve, page 72

  3 pkgs. (8 oz. each) frozen
    Brussels sprouts
  3 cups julienne fresh carrots
  2 tablespoons hot water
¼ cup butter or margarine
  1 tablespoon white wine
½ teaspoon dried mint leaves

Serves 6 to 8

Place Brussels sprouts, carrots
and water in 3-qt. casserole;
cover. Microwave at High 15 to
20 minutes, or until carrots are
tender and Brussels sprouts
heated, stirring twice during
cooking to break apart. Drain.
Set aside.

Place butter, wine and mint in
2-cup measure or small bowl.
Microwave at High 1 to 1½
minutes, or until melted and
bubbly. Pour over vegetables,
tossing to coat. If necessary,
microwave at High 1 to 2
minutes, or until reheated.

Marinated
Brussels Sprouts
Freezer Cocktail Party, page 32

  1 pkg. (16 oz.) frozen Brussels
    sprouts*
½ cup olive oil
¼ cup white wine vinegar
  2 tablespoons lemon juice
½ teaspoon salt
½ teaspoon sugar
¼ teaspoon dried oregano
    leaves
⅛ to ¼ teaspoon garlic powder
⅛ teaspoon dried basil leaves
  6 peppercorns

Serves 10 to 12

Place Brussels sprouts in 2-qt.
casserole. Mix remaining
ingredients in 2-cup measure;
pour over Brussels sprouts.
Cover. Microwave at High 6 to 9
minutes, or until Brussels
sprouts are tender. Refrigerate
overnight, stirring once or twice
to coat.

Let stand at room temperature
while preparing meal. Serve at
room temperature.

*If Brussels sprouts have ice
crystals on them, rinse with
warm water; drain.

Corn on the Cob ▶

Labor Day, page 62

10 to 12 ears corn in husk

Herb Butter, below

Serves 10 to 12

Arrange 1 to 4 unhusked ears of corn on oven floor with space between. No preparation is needed. Microwave following times in chart. Let stand 5 minutes. Husk corn after standing. Using paper napkin, hold corn with tip pointing down. Pull back leaves carefully to avoid steam. Grasp silk in other hand and pull sharply.

Amt.	Microwave Time	Procedure
1	3 to 5 min.	Turn over;
2	4 to 9 min.	rearrange after half the time.
3	9 to 12 min.	Turn over;
4	10 to 17 min.	rearrange every 4 minutes.

Herb Butter for Corn

1 cup butter or margarine
1 teaspoon dried chives
½ teaspoon sugar
½ teaspoon salt
¼ teaspoon pepper
2 tablespoons grated
   Parmesan cheese

Makes about 1 cup

In 1-qt. casserole combine butter, chives, sugar, salt and pepper. Microwave at High 2 to 3 minutes, or until butter melts, stirring after half the time. Stir in Parmesan cheese. Serve with corn on the cob.

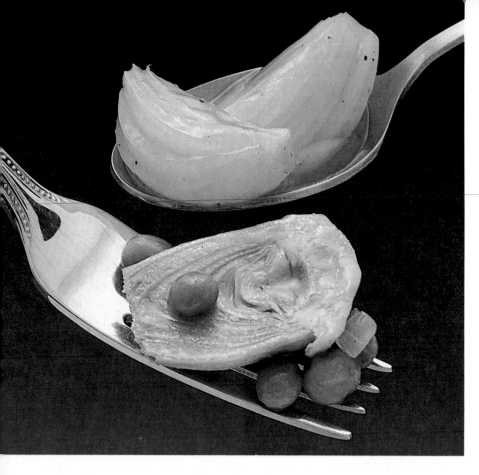

Black-Eyed Peas
New Year's Day, page 48

  2 lbs. dried black-eyed peas
    Hot water
  5 cups hot water
  8 oz. salt pork, cut into ½-in.
    cubes
  1 cup chopped onion
  1 clove garlic, minced
  ½ teaspoon salt
  ⅛ to ¼ teaspoon cayenne
  1 bay leaf

Serves 20

In 5-qt. casserole combine peas and enough hot water to cover peas. Microwave at High 10 to 14 minutes, or until water boils. Microwave at High 2 minutes longer. Let stand 1 hour.

Drain peas. Add 5 cups hot water, the salt pork, onion, garlic, salt, cayenne and bay leaf; cover. Microwave at High 10 minutes. Reduce power to 50% (Medium). Microwave 1 to 1¾ hours, or until peas are tender, stirring every 20 to 30 minutes during cooking. Remove bay leaf.

For thicker peas: After half the cooking time, remove 1 cup of peas; mash. Return to casserole and continue microwaving.

Advance preparation: Prepare the day before and refrigerate. To reheat, microwave at High 20 to 30 minutes, or until hot, stirring 2 or 3 times during cooking. Prepared or reheated peas can stand up to 1 hour, covered, before serving.

Glazed Onions ▲
Christmas Day, page 74

  3 tablespoons packed brown
    sugar
  1 tablespoon cornstarch
  ¼ teaspoon dry mustard
  ¼ teaspon salt
  ⅛ teaspoon pepper
  ⅓ cup hot water
  3 tablespoons cider vinegar
  8 small white onions, cut into
    quarters

Serves 6 to 8

In 2-cup measure mix brown sugar, cornstarch, mustard, salt and pepper. Gradually add water and vinegar, stirring until smooth. Microwave at High 1½ to 2½ minutes, or until slightly thickened, stirring once.

Place onions in 1-qt. casserole. Pour sauce over onions, stirring to coat; cover. Microwave at High 5 to 8 minutes, or until tender-crisp, stirring 2 or 3 times during cooking. Let stand 5 minutes.

Advance preparation: Onions can stand, covered, 1 hour.

Peas & Artichokes ▲
Dinner Party for Eight, page 16

  2 pkgs. (9 oz. each) frozen
    artichoke hearts
  ¼ cup butter or margarine
  3 tablespoons chopped onion
  ¼ teaspoon salt
    Dash pepper
  2 pkgs. (10½ oz. each) frozen
    green peas

Serves 8

Place artichoke packages in oven. Microwave at High 4½ to 7 minutes, or until packages are slightly warm, rearranging once. Drain well; set aside.

Microwave butter and onion at High 2 to 3½ minutes, or until onion is tender. Add salt and pepper. Stir in artichoke hearts, tossing to coat. Set aside.

Place peas in 1½-qt. casserole. Microwave, covered, at High 6 to 9 minutes, or until tender. Drain. Stir in artichokes. Microwave, covered, at High 2 to 4 minutes, or until heated through.

Buttered Potato Wedges ▲
Father's Day, page 58

⅓ cup butter or margarine
⅛ teaspoon pepper
2 lbs. baking potatoes
3 tablespoons grated
    Parmesan cheese
¾ cup cut-up green onions, ½-
    to ¾-in. pieces

Serves 4 to 6

Place butter in 1-cup measure. Microwave at High 45 to 60 seconds, or until melted. Stir in pepper. Cut each potato into quarters. Arrange potato wedges on 12-in. plate or large microwave baking sheet. Brush with half of butter. Cover with plastic wrap.

Microwave at High 5 minutes. Rearrange potatoes. Brush with remaining butter. Sprinkle with cheese and green onions; cover. Microwave at High 7 to 13 minutes, or until potatoes are just fork tender. Let stand, covered, 5 to 6 minutes.

Advance preparation: Cover with foil during standing time. Potatoes will hold temperature for 30 minutes before serving when covered with foil.

New Potatoes ▶
Easter, page 54

2½ lbs. small red potatoes
  ½ teaspoon salt
  ¼ cup hot water

Serves 8

Peel narrow strip from center of potatoes. In 3-qt. casserole dissolve salt in water. Add potatoes; cover. Microwave at High 6 to 12 minutes, or until tender. Let stand 5 minutes.

Advance preparation: Potatoes can stand, covered, 20 minutes.

Braised Green Peppers
Foreign Affair: Spanish, page 44

6 large green peppers
1 medium onion, thinly sliced
    and separated into rings
1 clove garlic, minced
1 teaspoon dried oregano
    leaves
2 tablespoons olive oil
1 teaspoon vinegar

Serves 6 to 8

Cut peppers in half lengthwise. Remove seeds and stems; rinse. Cut into long ½-in. wide strips. In 3-qt. casserole combine all ingredients; cover. Microwave at High 8 to 14 minutes, or until peppers are tender-crisp, stirring twice.

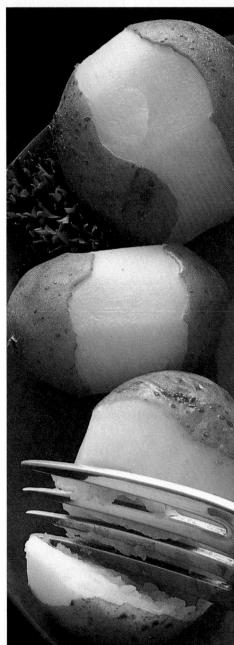

◀ Potato Rosettes

Freezer Buffet, page 36

1½ teaspoons salt, divided
 ½ cup hot water
  9 large baking potatoes,
     peeled and quartered
 ½ cup butter or margarine
 ½ cup dairy sour cream
  2 tablespoons grated
     Parmesan cheese
  2 cups milk
  1 teaspoon dried chives
     Paprika

Makes 4½ to 5 dozen

How to Microwave Potato Rosettes

Dissolve ½ teaspoon salt in water. In 3-qt. casserole combine potatoes and salted water; cover. Microwave at High 21 to 28 minutes, or until tender, stirring twice. Drain and mash.

Mix potatoes, butter, sour cream, cheese and 1 teaspoon salt in large bowl.

Add milk gradually, beating at high speed of electric mixer until smooth. Stir in chives.

Spoon potatoes into pastry bag using number 6 star tip. Squeeze into 2- to 2½-in. rosettes on wax paper-lined baking sheets. Sprinkle with paprika. Freeze 3 hours or overnight.

Place in plastic bags. Freeze up to 1 week. To heat, place 15 rosettes on 12-in. plate; cover with wax paper. Microwave at 70% (Medium-High) 5 minutes.

Rearrange rosettes with spatula so that those around outer edge are in center; cover. Microwave at 70% (Medium-High) 2 to 6 minutes, or until heated. Repeat with remaining rosettes.

116

Twice Baked Potatoes ▲
Christmas Eve, page 72

4 large baking potatoes
6 slices bacon
¼ cup butter or margarine
2 green onions, chopped
½ cup milk
½ teaspoon salt
⅛ teaspoon pepper
  Paprika

Serves 6 to 8

Pierce well-scrubbed potatoes twice. Place 1 inch apart on paper towel in oven. Microwave at High 10½ to 12½ minutes, or until just softened, rearranging and turning over after half the cooking time. Let stand, covered with a bowl, 5 minutes.

Place bacon on paper towel-lined plate. Cover with paper towel. Microwave at High 5 to 6 minutes, or until crisp. Drain on paper towel; crumble. Place butter and onion in 2-qt. casserole; cover. Microwave at High 1½ to 2 minutes, or until butter is melted and onion tender.

Cut potatoes in half lengthwise. Scoop out center; place in casserole with onion-butter and bacon. Add milk, salt and pepper; mash until fluffy. Spoon into potato shells. Arrange on paper towel-lined baking sheet. Sprinkle with paprika. Microwave at High 3 to 7 minutes, or until heated, rotating ½ turn. Garnish with additional chopped green onion, if desired.

Sweet Potato Casserole
Thanksgiving, page 66

4 lbs. sweet potatoes or yams
⅓ cup butter or margarine
⅓ cup packed brown sugar
1 teaspoon ground cinnamon
½ teaspoon salt
3 eggs, slightly beaten
⅓ cup fresh orange juice*
3 tablespoons brandy
2 tablespoons grated orange peel
1 tablespoon grated lemon peel

Serves 12 to 14

Pierce potatoes 2 or 3 times. Place all in oven on paper towel. Microwave at High 12 to 18 minutes, or until soft when pierced with fork, rearranging once or twice. Let stand 5 minutes. Remove peel; discard.

Melt butter at High 45 to 60 seconds. In large bowl mash potatoes with butter. Mix in remaining ingredients. Spoon into 2-qt. casserole. Microwave at High 5 minutes; stir. Reduce power to 70% (Medium-High). Microwave 8 to 12 minutes, or until heated. Garnish with orange slices and almonds, if desired.

*Use orange juice from Cranberry-Orange Relish recipe if preparing Thanksgiving menu.

Advance preparation: Covered with foil, casserole remains hot 45 minutes. If refrigerated, reheat casserole at 70% (Medium-High), 9 to 15 minutes.

Fruit-Filled Squash Rings
Christmas Day, page 74

2 or 3 whole acorn squash
1 can (16 oz.) whole-berry cranberry sauce
1 cup chopped dried apple
¼ cup chopped nuts
2 teaspoons cornstarch
1 teaspoon grated orange peel

Serves 6 to 8

Wash squash; pierce deeply several times with fork. Place on paper towel in oven. Microwave at High 13 to 15 minutes, or until squash feels soft and yields slightly to pressure, rotating and turning once. Let stand 15 minutes.

In 1-qt. casserole mix remaining ingredients. Microwave at High 3 to 6 minutes, or until thickened, stirring after half the time. Cool.

Cut squash into 1- to 1½-in. rings; discard seeds. Place rings in two 12 × 8-in. baking dishes or on baking sheet; cover. Microwave at High 4 to 7 minutes, or until squash is tender throughout. Place rings on serving plate; fill with cranberry sauce.

◄ Vegetables Provencal
Cocktail Party Buffet, page 18

   4 cups small cauliflowerets
   2 cups sliced carrots
   ¼ cup water
   ½ cup sliced pitted black olives
   2 medium green peppers, cut
      into thin strips
   1 bottle (8 oz.) Italian salad
      dressing
   2 tablespoons white wine
   1 teaspoon sugar

                  Serves 8

In 2-qt. casserole combine cauliflowerets, carrots and water. Cover. Microwave at High 6 to 11 minutes, or until cauliflowerets are tender-crisp, stirring after half the cooking time. Drain.

Add remaining ingredients. Cover and refrigerate at least 4 hours, stirring occasionally. Remove vegetables with a slotted spoon to serving dish.

Steamed Vegetables
Foreign Affair: Oriental, page 38

   3 medium zucchini, cut into
      ¼-in. diagonal pieces
   1½ cups diagonally sliced
      carrots
   1 medium green pepper, cut
      into ½-in. strips
   1 cup green onion slices,
      1-in.
   1 tablespoon cornstarch
   1 teaspoon salt
   ½ teaspoon sugar
   ⅛ teaspoon pepper
   1 tablespoon soy sauce
   1 tablespoon sherry

             Serves 6 to 8

In 2-qt. casserole combine zucchini, carrots, green pepper and green onions; cover. Microwave at High 5 minutes.

Blend remaining ingredients in small bowl. Stir into vegetables. Microwave at High 4½ to 8 minutes, or until sauce is slightly thickened and vegetables are tender-crisp, stirring once or twice. Serve with additional soy sauce, if desired.

Vegetables Mornay ►
Freezer Buffet, page 36

   6 to 8 carrots, cut into ¼-in.
      diagonal slices
   ¼ cup hot water
   1 pkg. (10 oz.) frozen
      chopped broccoli
   1 pkg. (10 oz.) frozen
      cauliflowerets
   1 can (8 oz.) whole
      mushrooms, drained
   ½ cup butter or margarine,
      divided
   2 tablespoons cornstarch
   1 teaspoon salt
   ¼ teaspoon pepper
  1½ cups milk
   2 tablespoons grated
      Parmesan cheese
   1 cup shredded Swiss
      cheese
   ½ cup seasoned croutons

          Serves 10 to 12

In 3-qt. casserole combine carrots and water; cover. Microwave at High 2 minutes. Add broccoli and cauliflowerets; cover. Microwave at High 7 to 12 minutes, or until tender; drain. Add mushrooms; cover and set aside.

Place 6 tablespoons butter in 4-cup measure. Microwave at High 30 to 60 seconds, or until melted. Stir in cornstarch, salt and pepper. Blend in milk. Microwave at High 4 to 6 minutes, or until thickened, stirring every minute. Stir in Parmesan and Swiss cheeses until cheeses melt and sauce is creamy.

Place 2 tablespoons butter in small bowl. Microwave at High 30 to 60 seconds, or until melted. Toss croutons with butter. Pour sauce over vegetable mixture. Stir gently to coat all vegetables. Microwave at High 4 to 5 minutes, or until sauce is bubbly and vegetables are hot. Stir in croutons during last minute of cooking.

Vegetable Chart

Vegetable	Amount	Microwave Time at High	Standing Time, Covered	Procedure
Artichokes				
Fresh	2	5½-8½ min.	3 min.	Trim and rinse artichokes. Wrap in plastic wrap.
	4	9½-14½ min.	3 min.	Arrange in oven with spaces between.
Frozen	9 oz. pkg.	5-6 min.	2 min.	1-qt. covered casserole with 2 tablespoons water. Stir after 2 minutes.
Asparagus				
Fresh	1 lb.	6½-9½ min.	3 min.	12 × 8-in. dish with ¼ cup water. Rearrange spears once.
Frozen	10 oz. pkg.	5-7 min.	3 min.	1-qt. covered casserole with 2 tablespoons water. Stir once.
Canned, spears & cuts	10 oz. can	2-4 min.		1-qt. covered casserole. Drain all but 1 tablespoon liquid. Stir once.
Beans				
Fresh, Green & Wax	1 lb.	7-13 min.	3 min.	Cut into 1½-in. pieces. 1½-qt. covered casserole with ¼ cup water. Stir once.
Frozen, Green & Wax	9 oz. pkg.	6-7 min.	3 min.	1-qt. covered casserole with 2 tablespoons water. Stir once.
Frozen, Lima	10 oz. pkg.	4-7 min.		1-qt. covered casserole with 2 tablespoons water. Stir once.
Canned, Green & Wax	15½ oz. can	2-4 min.		1-qt. covered casserole. Drain all but 2 tablespoons liquid. Stir once.
Canned, Lima	15-16 oz. can	2-3 min.	1 min.	1-qt. covered casserole. Drain all but 2 tablespoons liquid. Stir once.
Canned, Pork & Beans	16 oz. can	3-4 min.		1-qt. covered casserole. Stir after first 2 minutes.
Beets				
Canned	16 oz. can	2-3 min.		1-qt. covered casserole. Drain all but 2 tablespoons liquid.
Broccoli				
Fresh, spears	1½ lbs.	8-12 min.	3 min.	12 × 8-in. dish with ½ cup water. Cover with plastic wrap. Rotate dish ½ turn once.
Frozen	10 oz. pkg.	5-7 min.	3 min.	1-qt. covered casserole with 2 tablespoons water. Stir once.
Brussels Sprouts				
Fresh	4 cups	4-8 min.	3 min.	1½-qt. covered casserole with ¼ cup water. Stir once.
Frozen	10 oz. pkg.	5-7 min.	3 min.	1-qt. covered casserole with 2 tablespoons water. Stir once.
Cabbage				
Shredded	1 lb.	7½-13½ min.	3 min.	¼-in. wide shreds. 1½-qt. covered casserole with 2 tablespoons water. Stir once.
Wedges	1 lb.	12½-15½ min.	2-3 min.	12 × 8-in. dish with ¼ cup water. Cover with plastic wrap. Rearrange wedges and rotate dish once.
Carrots				
Fresh, slices, ⅛-in.	2 cups	4-7 min.	3 min.	1-qt. covered casserole with 2 tablespoons water. Stir once.
Frozen, sliced	2 cups	4-7 min.	3 min.	1-qt. covered casserole with 2 tablespoons water. Stir once.

Vegetable	Amount	Microwave Time at High	Standing Time, Covered	Procedure
Cauliflower				
Fresh, whole	1 lb.	5½-7½ min.	3 min.	Wrap in plastic wrap. Turn over after 3 minutes.
Fresh, flowerets	2 cups	4-7 min.	3 min.	1-qt. covered casserole with 2 tablespoons water. Stir once.
Frozen	10 oz. pkg.	5-7 min.	3 min.	1-qt. covered casserole with 2 tablespoons water. Stir once.
Corn				
Fresh, husked	2 ears	4½-10 min.	5 min.	12×8-in. dish with ¼ cup water. Cover with plastic wrap. Turn over and rearrange once or twice.
	4 ears	7½-16 min.	5 min.	
Frozen, cob	2 small ears	5½-7½ min.	3 min.	12×8-in. dish with 2 tablespoons water. Cover with plastic wrap. Turn over and rearrange once.
Frozen, whole kernel	10 oz. pkg.	4-6 min.	3 min.	1-qt. covered casserole with 2 tablespoons water. Stir once.
Canned, whole kernel	16 oz. can	2-3 min.		1-qt. covered casserole. Drain all but 2 tablespoons liquid. Stir once.
Okra				
Frozen, whole	10 oz. pkg.	5-6 min.	2 min.	1-qt. covered casserole with 2 tablespoons water. Stir every 2 minutes.
Frozen, sliced	10 oz. pkg.	5-7 min.	2 min.	1-qt. covered casserole with 2 tablespoons water. Stir every 2 minutes.
Canned	14½ oz. can	3-4 min.		1-qt. covered casserole. Drain all but 2 tablespoons liquid. Stir once or twice.
Peas, Black-Eyed				
Frozen	10 oz. pkg.	8-9 min.	2 min.	1-qt. covered casserole with ¼ cup water. Stir every 2 minutes.
Peas, Garden				
Fresh	2 cups	5-8 min.	3 min.	1-qt. covered casserole with ¼ cup water. Stir once.
Frozen	10 oz. pkg.	4-6 min.	2 min.	1-qt. covered casserole with 2 tablespoons water. Stir once.
Canned	16 oz. can	2-3 min.		1-qt. covered casserole. Drain all but 2 tablespoons liquid. Stir once.
Pea Pods				
Fresh	¼ lb.	2-4 min.	2 min.	1-qt. covered casserole with 2 tablespoons water.
Frozen	6 oz. pkg.	3-4 min.	2 min.	1-qt. covered casserole with 2 tablespoons water. Stir once.
Potatoes				
Baked	2 med.	5-7 min.	5-10 min.	Prick potatoes. Place on paper towel. Turn over and rearrange after half the cooking time. Let stand wrapped in foil.
	4 med.	10½-12½ min.	5-10 min.	
Boiled	4 med.	7-9 min.	3 min.	Peel and quarter potatoes. 1- to 1½-qt. covered casserole with ¼ cup water and ½ teaspoon salt. Rearrange once. Drain.
Spinach				
Fresh	1 lb.	5-8 min.	3 min.	3-qt. covered casserole with 2 tablespoons water. Stir once.
Canned	15 oz. can	3-4 min.		1-qt. covered casserole. Drain all liquid. Stir once.
Squash				
Acorn Squash, fresh	1	8½-11½ min.	5-10 min.	Cut in half; wrap with plastic wrap. Rotate and rearrange halves after half the cooking time.
	2	13-16 min.	5-10 min.	
Zucchini, fresh ¼-in. slices	2 cups	2½-6½ min.	3 min.	2-qt. covered casserole with 2 tablespoons butter or margarine. Stir once.
Frozen, mashed	12 oz. pkg.	5½-8 min.		1-qt. covered casserole. Break apart after 2 minutes, then stir at 2 minute intervals.
Sweet Potatoes				
Baked (5-7 oz.)	2 whole	5-9 min.	3 min.	Wash, prick, place on paper towel. Rearrange once during cooking.
	4 whole	8-13 min.	3 min.	

Rice

◄ Wild Rice Medley
Adult Birthday Party, page 24

1½ cups uncooked wild rice
5 cups hot water
½ cup chopped onion
½ cup finely chopped celery
¼ cup butter or margarine
8 oz. fresh mushrooms, sliced
1 tablespoon instant chicken
   bouillon granules

Serves 8

Rinse rice in wire strainer under cold running water. In 5-qt. casserole combine rice and hot water; cover. Microwave at High 30 to 35 minutes, or until rice is tender and fluffy, stirring every 10 minutes. Let rice stand, covered, 15 minutes.

In 2-qt. casserole combine onion, celery and butter; cover. Microwave at High 2 to 4 minutes, or until onion is tender-crisp. Stir in mushrooms and bouillon granules. Microwave at High 2 to 3 minutes, or until heated. Drain and rinse rice. Mix with vegetables; cover. Microwave at High 3 to 4 minutes, or until heated.

Long Grain Rice

Freezer Impromptu Dinner, page 28

⅔ cup uncooked long grain
    rice
½ teaspoon salt
1⅓ cups hot water
1 tablespoon butter or
    margarine

                Serves 2

Combine all ingredients in 1-qt. casserole; cover. Microwave at High 3 minutes. Reduce power to 50% (Medium). Microwave 7 to 10 minutes, or until liquid is absorbed. Let stand 5 minutes. Wrap, label and freeze no longer than 6 weeks.

To serve, place rice in 1-qt. casserole; cover. Microwave at High 5 to 10 minutes, or until hot, stirring twice. Let stand, covered, up to 30 minutes.

Shrimp & Rice

Foreign Affair: Oriental, page 38

2¾ cups hot water
¼ cup soy sauce
1½ cups uncooked long grain
    rice
1 tablespoon instant chicken
    bouillon granules
¼ cup chopped green onion
1 egg, beaten
1 can (4½ oz.) tiny shrimp,
    drained

             Serves 6 to 8

In 3-qt. casserole combine water, soy sauce, rice and bouillon granules. Microwave, covered, at High 5 minutes. Reduce power to 50% (Medium). Microwave 16 to 21 minutes, or until liquid is absorbed. Stir in green onion. Let stand, covered, 5 minutes.

Mix in egg. Microwave at High 2 to 4 minutes, or until egg is set, stirring once. Stir in shrimp.

Advance preparation: Rice can stand, covered, 20 to 25 minutes. Rice can also be made early in the day and refrigerated. To serve, microwave, covered, at High 10 to 15 minutes, or until heated, stirring once or twice.

Saffron Rice

Foreign Affair: Spanish, page 44

¼ cup chopped green pepper
1 large clove garlic, minced
1 tablespoon olive oil
¼ teaspoon ground saffron
3 cups hot water
1½ cups uncooked long grain
    rice

            Serves 6 to 8

In 3-qt. casserole combine green pepper, garlic, olive oil and saffron. Microwave at High 2 minutes. Add water and rice.

Microwave, covered, at High 5 minutes. Reduce power to 50% (Medium). Microwave 12 to 17 minutes, or until rice is tender and liquid is absorbed. Let stand 5 to 10 minutes. Fluff with fork.

NOTE: Because of the high cost of saffron, Parslied Rice, below, is offered as an alternative to complement the Spanish menu.

Parslied Rice

1 large onion, chopped
1 tablespoon olive oil or butter
¾ teaspoon dried basil leaves
¼ teaspoon dried thyme leaves
3 cups hot water
1½ cups uncooked long grain
    rice
¾ cup snipped fresh parsley
1½ teaspoons salt
¼ teaspoon pepper

            Serves 6 to 8

Place onion, olive oil, basil and thyme in 3-qt. casserole. Microwave, covered, at High 2½ to 4 minutes, or until onion is tender. Stir in remaining ingredients; cover.

Microwave at High 5 minutes. Reduce power to 50% (Medium). Microwave 12 to 17 minutes, or until rice is tender and liquid is absorbed. Let stand 5 to 10 minutes. Fluff with fork.

Riz Indienne

Foreign Affair: East Indian, page 42

½ cup chopped onion
2 tablespoons butter or
    margarine
3½ cups hot water
2 cups uncooked long grain
    rice
1 cup blanched almonds
1 cup raisins
2 tablespoons instant chicken
    bouillon granules
1 teaspoon salt
½ teaspoon pepper

            Serves 6 to 8

Microwave onion and butter in 3-qt. casserole at High 2 to 4 minutes, or until onion is tender. Stir in remaining ingredients; cover. Microwave at High 8 minutes. Reduce power to 50% (Medium). Microwave 15 to 19 minutes, or until rice is tender and liquid is absorbed. Let stand, covered, 10 minutes. Fluff with fork.

Saffron Brown Rice

Simple Dinner for Four, page 14

1 cup quick-cooking brown
    rice
1 cup hot water
½ cup dry white wine
1 small onion, chopped
2 tablespoons butter or
    margarine
1 teaspoon instant chicken
    bouillon granules
½ teaspoon salt
⅛ teaspoon ground saffron
    Dash pepper

            Serves 4

Combine all ingredients in 2-qt. casserole. Microwave, covered, at High 5 minutes. Reduce power to 50% (Medium). Microwave 7 to 12 minutes, or until liquid is absorbed. Let stand, covered, 5 minutes.

NOTE: Because of the high cost of saffron, Parslied Rice, opposite, is offered as an alternative to complement the Simple Dinner menu.

Fruits

◄ Fruit With Raspberry Dip
Spring Open House, page 20

¼ cup shredded coconut
2 tablespoons finely chopped
    pecans
1 cup dairy sour cream
¼ cup raspberry preserves
2 tablespoons milk
    Fresh fruit dippers (apple,
    orange and pear wedges,
    banana pieces, straw-
    berries, grapes, melon
    balls)
    Lemon juice

Serves 20

Mix coconut, pecans, sour
cream, preserves and milk.
Toss apple, pear and banana
pieces in lemon juice. Arrange
fruit around bowl of dip on bed
of ice. Serve with cocktail picks.

Baked Grapefruit
Mother's Day, page 56

2 large grapefruit
½ cup dairy sour cream
2 tablespoons packed brown
    sugar
4 maraschino cherries

Serves 4

Cut grapefruit in half. With thin
sharp knife, cut around each
section to loosen fruit from
membrane. Place in 8 × 8-in.
baking dish or individual serving
dishes. Blend sour cream and
brown sugar thoroughly; spread
one-fourth on top of each
grapefruit half. Microwave at
High 2 to 4½ minutes, or until
warm, rearranging once. Top
each with maraschino cherry.

Fruit Kabobs ▲
Midnight Supper, page 26

1 tablespoon cornstarch
⅛ teaspoon ground cinnamon
¼ cup lemon juice
¼ cup orange juice
3 tablespoons honey
1 medium apple, cut into 1-in.
    cubes

1 can (8 oz.) pineapple
    chunks, drained
1 can (8 oz.) mandarin orange
    sections, drained
1 medium banana, cut into
    ½-in. slices
6 wooden skewers, 6-in.

Serves 6

In 2-cup measure mix cornstarch, cinnamon, lemon juice, orange
juice and honey. Microwave at High 1½ to 3½ minutes, or until
thick, stirring once or twice.

Alternate apple, pineapple, orange and banana on skewers to fill
each skewer. Brush with glaze. Refrigerate. Brush with glaze again
before serving.

Spiced Apple Relish ▲
Dinner Party for Eight, page 16

6 cups chopped apples
⅓ cup chopped onion
¼ cup sugar
¼ cup chopped spiced
   peaches or raisins, optional
¼ cup water
¼ teaspoon ground cloves
   Dash salt

Makes 2½ to 3 cups

Combine all ingredients in 2-qt.
casserole; cover. Microwave at
High 10 to 15 minutes, or until
apples are soft, stirring once or
twice. Mash apples. Serve with
pork or poultry.

Advance preparation: Prepare
relish the day before; refrigerate.
Let stand at room temperature
while preparing meal. Serve at
room temperature.

Cranberry-Orange Relish ▲
Thanksgiving, page 66

2 oranges
8 cups fresh cranberries
1⅓ cups sugar
¼ cup chopped crystallized
   ginger
½ cup chopped pecans,
   optional

Serves 12 to 14

Squeeze juice from oranges;
refrigerate in covered container
for other use. Remove pulp from
orange peels; discard. Cut
peels in quarters; finely grind in
food processor. Add half the
cranberries and continue
processing until ground. Repeat
with remaining cranberries.

In 3-qt. bowl mix cranberries,
sugar and ginger. Stir in
pecans. Refrigerate.

NOTE: A blender or grinder can
be substituted for food processor.

Fresh Fruit Chutney ▲
Foreign Affair: East Indian, page 42

3 large apples, peeled and
   chopped
1 mango, peeled and
   chopped
1 medium onion, chopped
1½ cups sugar
1 cup raisins
½ cup cider vinegar
1 teaspoon salt
½ teaspoon dry mustard

Makes 4 cups

Combine all ingredients in 3-qt.
casserole. Microwave, uncovered, at High 20 to 30 minutes,
or until fruit is very soft and
liquid is slightly thickened,
stirring 2 or 3 times during
cooking time.

Remove fruit from liquid and
coarsely mash. Return fruit to
liquid. Cover and refrigerate.
Store no longer than 2 weeks.

Poached Oranges ▶

Foreign Affair: Spanish, page 44

7 large oranges
½ cup sangria
½ teaspoon grated lemon
　　peel

Serves 6 to 8

Advance preparation: Prepare early in day; refrigerate.

How to Microwave Poached Oranges

Slice off ends of fruit. Using a sawing motion, peel in spiral. Remove membrane, leaving as much fruit as possible.

Hold fruit over bowl to catch juice. Cut to center between fruit segment and dividing membrane with sharp knife.

Place orange sections in 1- to 1½-qt. casserole. Combine sangria and lemon peel. Pour over orange sections; cover.

Microwave at High 2 to 5 minutes, or until heated, stirring once or twice during cooking time. Serve warm or cold.

127

Salads

Lettuce Cups

Valentine's Day, page 50

Dressing:
 2 slices bacon, cut into ½-in.
    pieces
    Vegetable oil
 ¼ cup red wine vinegar
 1 teaspoon grated Parmesan
    cheese
 ½ teaspoon dried parsley flakes
 ½ teaspoon dried basil leaves

 ¼ teaspoon salt
 ⅛ teaspoon dry mustard
    Dash pepper

Salad:
 1 head iceberg lettuce
    Chopped tomato
    Chopped hard cooked egg
    Croutons

Serves 2

Place bacon in 2-cup measure. Microwave at High 1½ to 2½ minutes, or until crisp, stirring once during cooking. Remove bacon; place on paper towel. Add enough vegetable oil to bacon drippings to measure ⅓ cup. Mix in remaining dressing ingredients. Microwave at High 30 to 45 seconds, or until hot. Stir in bacon.

Remove outer leaves from head of lettuce; arrange on plate to form cups. Tear enough remaining lettuce into bite-size pieces to fill lettuce cups. Sprinkle with chopped tomato, chopped hard cooked egg and croutons. Spoon hot dressing over top.

Shredded Lettuce Salad ▼

After the Game, page 22

 1 large head iceberg lettuce,
    shredded
 2 cups shredded Cheddar
    cheese
 2 medium tomatoes, chopped
 ½ cup chopped onion
 ½ cup sliced pitted black olives
 ¼ cup plus 2 tablespoons
    taco sauce
 ¼ teaspoon cumin
 1½ cups dairy sour cream

Serves 10 to 12

On large round platter or in large bowl layer lettuce, cheese, tomatoes, onion and olives. In small bowl mix taco sauce and cumin. Microwave at High 45 seconds to 1½ minutes, or until heated. Stir in sour cream. Serve with lettuce salad.

◄ Parmesan Lettuce Wedges

Christmas Day, page 74

 1 cup vegetable oil
 ½ cup red wine vinegar
 3 tablespoons grated
    Parmesan cheese
 1 clove garlic, minced
 ½ teaspoon sugar
 ¼ teaspoon dry mustard
 ¼ teaspoon pepper
 1 large head iceberg lettuce,
    cut into 6 to 8 wedges

Serves 6 to 8

In 4-cup measure or medium bowl mix all ingredients except lettuce. Serve over lettuce wedges. Garnish with cherry tomatoes, if desired.

Tossed Salad

Freezer Dinner, page 34

Iceberg lettuce, torn into
    bite-size pieces
Tomato wedges
Cucumber slices
Radish slices
Dried oregano leaves

Serves 2 to 12

Toss all ingredients in bowl. Serve with oil and red wine vinegar or Italian salad dressing, if desired.

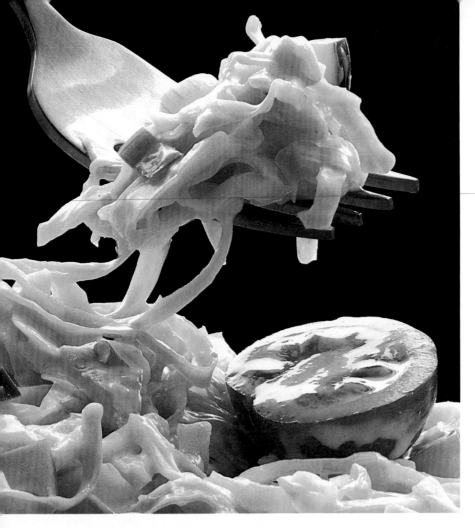

Lemon-Ginger Fruit Salad
New Year's Eve, page 46

  ¾ cup sugar
  1 tablespoon cornstarch
  ¾ cup water
1½ teaspoons grated lemon
    peel
  3 tablespoons fresh lemon
    juice
1½ teaspoons grated, peeled
    gingerroot
  8 to 10 cups cut-up fresh fruit
    (apples, pears, apricots,
    pineapple, oranges,
    cherries, firm bananas)

                Serves 6 to 8

Combine sugar and cornstarch in small bowl or 4-cup measure. Stir in water, lemon peel, lemon juice and gingerroot. Microwave at High 4 to 6 minutes, or until thick and translucent, stirring once or twice. Pour over fruit.

Advance preparation: Can be prepared the day before the party. Cover and refrigerate. Add cherries and bananas just before serving.

Confetti Slaw ▲
Saint Patrick's Day, page 52

  1 medium head cabbage,
    shredded (12 cups)
  1 cup chopped tomato or
    cherry tomatoes, cut in half
  2 cups chopped green pepper
  1 cup coarsley chopped
    cucumber
  ½ cup sliced green onion
  1 cup salad dressing or
    mayonnaise
  1 cup dairy sour cream
  1 tablespoon snipped fresh
    parsley
  1 teaspoon sugar
  1 teaspoon salt
  ½ teaspoon garlic salt

                Serves 6 to 8

In large bowl combine cabbage, tomato, green pepper, cucumber and onion. In small bowl mix remaining ingredients. Pour over vegetables, tossing to coat. Refrigerate 8 hours or overnight.

Zucchini Slaw
Labor Day, page 62

  5 cups shredded cabbage
  3 cups shredded zucchini
  1 cup grated carrot
  ½ cup chopped onion
  ¼ cup sugar
  ¼ cup vegetable oil
  ¼ cup vinegar
  ¼ teaspoon celery seed
  ⅛ teaspoon pepper

             Serves 10 to 12

In large bowl toss together cabbage, zucchini, carrot and onion. Set aside. In 4-cup measure mix sugar, oil, vinegar, celery seed and pepper. Microwave at High 1 to 1½ minutes, or until boiling. Pour over vegetables; toss to coat.

Advance preparation: Prepare carrot, cabbage and onion. Store each in separate plastic bag. Before serving, shred zucchini and prepare dressing. Toss vegetables with dressing.

Citrus Salad
Freezer Dinner, page 30

  2 oranges, peeled and
    sectioned, page 127
  1 grapefruit, peeled and
    sectioned, page 127
  2 tablespoons water
  2 tablespoons sherry
  1 tablespoon honey
  1 teaspoon cornstarch
  ⅛ teaspoon dried basil leaves

                 Serves 2

In small serving bowl combine orange and grapefruit sections. In 1-cup measure mix remaining ingredients. Microwave at High 45 seconds to 1½ minutes, or until thickened, stirring after half the time. Pour over fruit sections; toss gently. Serve warm or chilled.

Spiced Pear Salad ▶
Easter, page 54

½ cup packed brown sugar
¼ cup sherry
 1 can (29 oz.) pear halves,
    drained and ¼ cup juice
    reserved
 1 tablespoon vinegar
¼ teaspoon ground cinnamon
¼ teaspoon ground nutmeg
    Dash ground cloves
½ pkg. (8 oz.) cream cheese
¼ cup chopped nuts
 8 lettuce leaves

Serves 8

In medium bowl mix brown
sugar, sherry, reserved juice,
vinegar, cinnamon, nutmeg and
cloves. Microwave at High 1 to
3 minutes, or until boiling,
stirring after half the time. Add
pear halves, stirring to coat.
Microwave at High 1 to 3
minutes, or until heated.
Refrigerate until chilled.

Cut cream cheese into eight
pieces. Shape into balls; roll in
nuts. For each serving, place 1
pear half on a lettuce leaf.
Spoon on sauce. Place cheese
ball in hollow of each pear half.

Advance preparation: Pears
and sauce can be made 1 to 2
days in advance. Assemble
salad before serving.

Orange-Endive Salad ▶
Simple Dinner for Four, page 14

 1 small head endive, torn into
    bite-size pieces
 1 small head leaf lettuce, torn
    into bite-size pieces
 2 oranges, peeled and
    sectioned, page 127
½ small red onion, cut into thin
    slices and separated into
    rings

Serves 4

Toss endive and lettuce
together. Add orange sections
and onion rings. Serve with
Italian dressing, if desired.

Advance preparation:
Assemble salad early in the
day. Refrigerate until serving.

Giardiniera Salad
Foreign Affair: Italian, page 40

3 medium unpeeled potatoes,
   cut into ½-in. cubes
1 medium onion, thinly sliced
   and separated into rings
3 medium zucchini, thinly
   sliced
1 cup sliced fresh mushrooms
½ cup sliced pitted black olives
1 jar (2 oz.) sliced pimientos,
   rinsed and drained
⅓ cup olive oil
3 tablespoons red wine vinegar
1 tablespoon lemon juice
2 teaspoons snipped fresh
   parsley
¾ teaspoon salt
½ teaspoon dried oregano
   leaves
½ teaspoon dried basil leaves

Serves 8

In 3-qt. casserole combine
potatoes and onion; cover.
Microwave at High 7 to 11
minutes, or until potatoes are
tender, stirring once or twice.
Add zucchini, mushrooms,
olives and pimiento.

In small bowl blend remaining
ingredients. Stir into vegetables.
Microwave, covered, at High 2
to 4 minutes, or until heated.
Stir. Refrigerate, covered, at
least 4 hours or overnight.

Antipasto
Foreign Affair: Italian, page 40

Green pepper strips
Green olives
Marinated artichoke hearts
Pickled mild cherry peppers
Anchovies
Provolone cheese
Ham and salami slices,
   rolled up

Serves 8

Arrange all ingredients on large
serving tray.

Advance preparation: Can be
arranged early in day. Cover
and refrigerate.

Creamy Potato Salad ▲
Fourth of July, page 60

1½ teaspoons salt, divided
½ cup hot water
12 medium potatoes, peeled
   and quartered
½ cup Italian salad dressing
¼ cup water
½ cup sugar
½ cup vinegar
½ teaspoon dry mustard
⅛ teaspoon white pepper

3 eggs, slightly beaten
1 tablespoon butter or
   margarine
¼ cup whipping cream
½ cup chopped celery
¼ cup chopped green onion
2 tablespoons snipped fresh
   parsley
4 hard cooked eggs, sliced,
   optional

Serves 12

Dissolve 1 teaspoon salt in ½ cup hot water. In 3-qt. casserole
combine potatoes and salted water; cover. Microwave at High 20
to 26 minutes, or until fork tender, stirring after half the time. Drain
and cut into slices or cubes. Toss with Italian salad dressing and
¼ cup water. Refrigerate until cool.

In 1-qt. casserole mix sugar, vinegar, ½ teaspoon salt, the mustard
and pepper. Microwave at High 2 to 4 minutes, or until boiling,
stirring after half the time. Stir a small amount of hot mixture into
beaten eggs; return slowly to hot mixture, stirring constantly.
Reduce power to 50% (Medium). Microwave 2 to 3 minutes, or
until thickened, stirring with wire whip every 30 seconds. Stir in
butter until melted. Refrigerate until chilled.

Mix cream into chilled dressing. Drain potatoes. Add celery, green
onion and parsley to potatoes. Pour dressing over vegetables,
tossing to coat. Garnish with sliced eggs. Chill.

Advance preparation: Potatoes can be prepared the night before.
Drain before adding dressing.

Mediterranean Salad ▶

Foreign Affair: Spanish, page 44

12 to 16 iceberg lettuce leaves
18 to 24 cooked or canned
    asparagus spears
12 to 16 strips anchovies
    Grated Parmesan cheese
    Olive oil
    Red wine vinegar

Serves 6 to 8

On each salad plate layer 2
lettuce leaves, 3 asparagus
spears and 2 strips anchovies.
Sprinkle with Parmesan cheese.
Garnish with black olives and
tomato wedges, if desired.
Serve with oil and vinegar.

Tomato Aspic

Fourth of July, page 60

  1 can (46 oz.) tomato juice,
    divided
1½ cups thinly sliced celery,
    divided
  ½ cup chopped onion
  ⅓ cup packed brown sugar
  3 tablespoons lemon juice
  ½ teaspoon salt
  4 whole cloves
  2 bay leaves
  3 envelopes unflavored
    gelatin
  1 medium green pepper,
    chopped
  1 cup grated carrot

Serves 12

Measure 1½ cups tomato juice
into 2-cup measure. Set aside.
In 2-qt. casserole combine
remaining juice, ½ cup celery,
the onion, brown sugar, lemon
juice, salt, cloves and bay
leaves; cover. Microwave at High
5 minutes. Reduce power to
50% (Medium). Microwave 10 to
15 minutes, or until flavors blend.

Stir gelatin into reserved 1½
cups tomato juice. Strain hot
tomato juice; stir in gelatin
mixture. Chill until thickened but
not set. Mix in 1 cup celery, the
green pepper and carrot. Pour
into 8- to 10-cup ring mold. Chill
until firm, about 4 hours.

◄ Wineberry Salad

Adult Birthday Party, page 24

1 cup cranberry cocktail juice
1 pkg. (3 oz.) raspberry gelatin mix
¼ cup sugar
¾ cup sangria
1 can (8 oz.) whole-berry cranberry sauce
1 cup chilled whipping cream, whipped
½ cup chopped pecans

Serves 8

Place cranberry juice in medium bowl. Microwave at High 2 to 3 minutes, or until boiling. Add gelatin, stirring to dissolve. Mix in sugar and sangria. Chill 1 hour, or until soft set. Fold in remaining ingredients. Pour into 6-cup mold. Chill 3 to 4 hours, or until set. Unmold onto plate.

Pineapple Cheese Salad

Christmas Eve, page 72

1 cup hot water
1 pkg. (3 oz.) lime gelatin mix
¾ cup cold water
1 can (8 oz.) crushed pineapple, drained
1 carton (4 oz.) frozen whipped dessert topping
½ cup ricotta cheese
½ cup chopped pecans
¼ cup chopped maraschino cherries

Serves 6 to 8

Pour hot water into medium bowl; cover. Microwave at High 1½ to 2 minutes, or until boiling. Stir in gelatin until dissolved. Mix in cold water. Refrigerate about 1 hour, or until slightly thickened. Stir in remaining ingredients. Pour into 4-cup mold. Chill until set. Unmold to serve.

Marinated Vegetable Salad

Foreign Affair: East Indian, page 42

4 large firm tomatoes, peeled and chopped
2 medium cucumbers, peeled and chopped
1 cup snipped fresh parsley
½ cup chopped green onion
1 or 2 cloves garlic, minced

2 tablespoons snipped fresh mint or 1 tablespoon dried mint flakes
¼ cup fresh lemon juice
¼ cup olive oil
¼ teaspoon salt
¼ teaspoon sugar

Serves 6 to 8

In medium bowl combine tomatoes, cucumbers, parsley, green onion, garlic and mint. Blend lemon juice, olive oil, salt and sugar. Pour over vegetables; stir to coat.

Advance preparation: Can be served immediately but flavors are enhanced by marinating overnight.

Jack-O'-Lantern Salad ►

Halloween, page 64

2 cups hot water
1 pkg. (6 oz.) orange gelatin
    mix
2 cups cold water
1 lb. carrots, shredded
    Curly endive
    Pitted dates
    Celery

Serves 12

How to Microwave Jack-O'-Lantern Salad

Pour hot water into medium bowl; cover. Microwave at High 4 to 6 minutes, or until boiling.

Stir in gelatin until dissolved. Add cold water. Chill 1 to 2 hours, or until soft set.

Stir in shredded carrots. Pour into 9-in. round cake dish. Chill until firm.

To serve, unmold gelatin onto plate covered with curly endive. Use dates to form pumpkin face and celery for stem.

Breads

◄ Soda Bread
Saint Patrick's Day, page 52

    1 to 2 tablespoons plain
       bread crumbs
    2 cups all-purpose flour
    1 cup raisins
    1 tablespoon sugar
    2 teaspoons baking soda
    ½ teaspoon salt
    2 tablespoons butter or
       margarine
  ⅔ cup buttermilk
    1 egg, beaten

Topping:
    1 tablespoon butter or
       margarine
    2 tablespoons plain bread
       crumbs
    1 tablespoon rolled oats
    ¼ teaspoon ground cinnamon

Makes 1 loaf

Lightly butter 1-qt. round
casserole. Coat with 1 to 2
tablespoons crumbs. In medium
bowl mix flour, raisins, sugar,
baking soda and salt. Place 2
tablespoons butter in small
bowl. Microwave at High 30 to
45 seconds, or until melted. Stir
the melted butter, buttermilk
and egg into flour mixture.
Spread in casserole.

Place 1 tablespoon butter in
small bowl. Microwave at High
30 to 45 seconds, or until
melted. Stir in 2 tablespoons
bread crumbs, the oats and
cinnamon. Spread over top of
bread. Place casserole in oven
on inverted saucer. With sharp
knife cut 1-in. deep "X" in top of
bread. Microwave at 70%
(Medium-High) 4½ to 9½
minutes, or until top springs
back when touched lightly,
rotating once or twice. Let stand
5 minutes. Remove from
casserole. Serve immediately or
cool on wire rack.

Orange Breakfast Ring

Mother's Day, page 56

Lemon wafer or graham
    cracker crumbs
¼ cup sugar
½ cup orange juice
 1 egg
 2 cups buttermilk baking mix
½ cup finely chopped pecans
½ cup orange marmalade
½ orange
 1 cup butter, softened
 1 teaspoon grated orange peel

Serves 4

Grease 10- or 12-cup ring cake dish; coat with crumbs. In medium bowl mix sugar, orange juice and egg. Beat in baking mix until blended. Stir in pecans and marmalade. Pour into dish.

Microwave at 50% (Medium) 5 minutes, rotating after half the time. Increase power to High. Microwave 1 to 5 minutes, or until no unbaked batter appears on bottom of dish. Let stand directly on counter 5 minutes. Invert onto plate.

Remove fruit from ½ orange to form a cup. Mix butter and orange peel. Spoon into orange cup. Place in center of warm coffee cake to serve.

Garlic Bread

Midnight Supper, page 26

 1 cup butter or margarine
¼ cup thinly sliced green
    onion
 2 cloves garlic, minced
 1 large loaf French bread

Serves 6

In 1-qt. casserole combine butter, green onion and garlic. Microwave at 30% (Medium-Low) for 30 to 60 seconds, or until butter is softened and spreadable. Stir to blend ingredients.

Slice bread lengthwise in half. Spread each half with softened butter. Reassemble bread; wrap in foil. Heat conventionally at 325° for 20 minutes, or until butter is melted.

Corn Bread Dressing

Thanksgiving, page 66

 2 pkgs. (8 oz. each) corn
    muffin mix
 8 slices bacon, cut into ½-in.
    pieces
 2 cups chopped celery
 1 cup chopped onion
½ cup butter or margarine
½ cup hot water, optional

 2 cans (10¾ oz. each)
    condensed chicken broth
 2 tablespoons snipped fresh
    parsley
 2 teaspoons poultry seasoning
 2 eggs, slightly beaten
 5 cups croutons

Serves 12 to 14

Prepare each corn muffin mix according to package directions. Pour into two 8 × 8-in. baking dishes. Place one dish on inverted saucer in oven. Microwave at 50% (Medium) 3 minutes, rotating dish once during cooking. Increase power to High. Microwave 1 to 3 minutes, or until top springs back when touched lightly with finger and no unbaked batter appears through bottom of dish. Repeat with remaining dish. Cool. Cut each into ½-in. cubes.

Place bacon in 5-qt. casserole. Cover with paper towel. Microwave at High 6 to 8 minutes, or until crisp, stirring 2 to 3 times during cooking. Drain; place on paper towel. In same casserole combine celery, onion and butter. Microwave at High 7 to 9 minutes, or until vegetables are tender. Stir in bacon, water, broth, parsley and poultry seasoning. Stir small amount of hot mixture into eggs, return gradually to hot mixture, stirring constantly. Mix in cubed cornbread and croutons. Microwave at High 7 to 10 minutes, or until some moisture has been absorbed and stuffing is hot.

Advance preparation: Stuffing can stand, covered, 30 to 40 minutes before serving.

Onion Caraway Bread

Father's Day, page 58

 2 envelopes (¼ oz. each)
    instant onion soup mix
 1 cup all-purpose flour
 1 cup whole wheat flour
 1 cup milk
½ cup butter or margarine,
    melted

 1 egg
 2 tablespoons packed dark
    brown sugar
 2 to 3 teaspoons caraway seed
 1 teaspoon baking powder
 1 teaspoon baking soda
 1 teaspoon salt

Makes 1 loaf

Generously butter 8 × 5-in. loaf dish. Use 1 envelope soup mix to coat bottom and side of greased dish. In medium bowl mix all ingredients except remaining soup mix. Pour into dish. Sprinkle remaining soup mix over batter. Shield ends with foil. Place dish in oven on inverted saucer.

Microwave at 50% (Medium) 8 minutes, rotating once. Remove foil. Increase power to High. Microwave 1 to 5 minutes, or until top is firm, rotating every 2 minutes. Let stand 5 minutes. Remove from dish; cool.

Advance preparation: Prepare the morning of the party.

Desserts

One Crust Pastry Shell

⅓ cup shortening
2 tablespoons butter or
   margarine, softened
1 cup all-purpose flour
½ teaspoon salt
3 tablespoons cold water
3 or 4 drops yellow food
   coloring, optional

Makes 9-in. pie shell

Cut shortening and butter into flour and salt using pastry blender until particles resemble coarse crumbs or small peas. Combine water and food coloring. Sprinkle over flour mixture while stirring with fork, until particles are just moist enough to cling together and form a ball. (You may not need all the water.)

Form dough into ball. Flatten to ½ inch on floured pastry cloth. Roll out to scant ⅛-in. thick circle, at least 2 inches larger than inverted pie plate. Fit loosely into pie plate. Do not stretch dough or it will shrink while microwaving. Let stand 10 minutes. Trim pastry overhang to generous ½ inch. Fold to form high-standing rim; flute. Prick with fork, continuously at bend and ½ inch apart on bottom and side.

Microwave at High 5 to 7 minutes, rotating plate ½ turn every 3 minutes. If crust bubbles, gently push back into shape. Check for doneness by looking through bottom of plate. Crust will not brown, but will appear dry and opaque.

Pecan Pie Pictured at left
Father's Day, page 58

1 egg, separated
1 microwaved 9-in. pastry
   shell, opposite
2 eggs
½ cup sugar
1 cup light corn syrup
¼ cup butter or margarine,
   melted
1 teaspoon vanilla
1 tablespoon all-purpose flour
¼ teaspoon salt
1½ cups broken pecan pieces

Makes 9-in. pie

Beat 1 egg yolk well. Brush cooked pastry shell with yolk to seal holes. Microwave at High 30 to 60 seconds, or until egg is set.

In medium mixing bowl blend remaining eggs and egg white with sugar. Mix in corn syrup, butter, vanilla, flour and salt until blended. Stir in pecans. Pour into pastry shell. Microwave at 50% (Medium) 13 to 17 minutes, or until filling is almost set, rotating ¼ turn every 4 minutes. Cool.

Variation:
Substitute walnuts for pecans.

Whole Wheat Pastry Shell With Cut-Outs

⅓ cup plus 2 tablespoons plus
   1½ teaspoons shortening
3 tablespoons butter or
   margarine, softened
¾ cup all-purpose flour
¾ cup whole wheat flour
⅓ cup finely chopped nuts
¾ teaspoon salt
¼ teaspoon ground nutmeg
3 tablespoons cold water
2 or 3 drops yellow food
   coloring, optional

Makes 9-in. pie shell
plus cut-outs

Cut shortening and butter into flours, nuts, salt and nutmeg using pastry blender until particles resemble coarse crumbs or small peas. Combine water and food coloring. Sprinkle over flour mixture while stirring with fork, until particles are just moist enough to cling together and form a ball. (You may not need all the water.) Reserve one-third dough for cut-outs.

Form remaining dough into ball. Flatten to ½ inch on floured pastry cloth. Roll out to scant ⅛-in. thick circle, at least 2 inches larger than inverted 9-in. pie plate. Fit loosely into pie plate. Do not stretch dough or it will shrink while microwaving. Let stand 10 minutes. Trim pastry overhang to generous ½ inch. Fold to form high-standing rim; flute. Prick with fork, continuously at bend and ½ inch apart on bottom and side.

Microwave at High 5 to 7 minutes, or until crust appears dry and opaque through bottom of pie plate, rotating two or three times during cooking. Cool.

For cut-outs, roll out reserved pastry to ⅛-in. thickness. Cut into 6 pieces with cookie cutter, or cut into 6- or 7-in. circle and prick with fork to outline 6 wedges. Arrange in circle on baking sheet or wax paper. Microwave at High 2 to 4 minutes until dry, rotating every minute. Watch closely. Loosen from wax paper while warm.

Grasshopper Pie
Saint Patrick's Day, page 52

¼ cup butter or margarine
1¼ cups fine chocolate cookie
    crumbs
36 large marshmallows
½ cup milk
¼ cup green crème de
    menthe
3 tablespoons white crème de
    cacao
1 cup chilled whipping cream

Makes 9-in. pie

Place butter in 9-in. pie plate. Microwave at High 45 seconds to 1½ minutes, or until melted. Blend in cookie crumbs. Press onto bottom and up side of pie plate. Microwave at High 1 to 3 minutes, or until hot, rotating once or twice. Set aside.

In 3-qt. casserole or large bowl combine marshmallows and milk. Microwave at High 3 to 5 minutes, or until marshmallows are melted, stirring often. Mix in crème de menthe and crème de cacao. Refrigerate 1 to 2 hours, or until cool, stirring 2 or 3 times.

When marshmallow mixture is cool, beat whipping cream in chilled bowl at high speed until soft peaks form. Fold marshmallow mixture into whipped cream. Pour into prepared shell. Chill at least 3 hours, or until set. Garnish with semi-sweet chocolate curls or additional chocolate cookie crumbs, if desired.

Frosty Pumpkin Pie ▲
Thanksgiving, page 66

¼ cup butter or margarine
1½ cups gingersnap crumbs
¼ cup packed brown sugar
½ teaspoon ground ginger
½ teaspoon ground nutmeg
½ teaspoon ground cinnamon
    Dash salt
1 cup canned pumpkin

1 teaspoon aromatic bitters,
    optional
1 pint (2 cups) butter pecan
    ice cream
¼ cup chopped pecans
1 carton (4½ oz.) frozen
    whipped topping,
    defrosted

Serves 6

Place butter in 9-in. pie plate. Microwave at High 1 to 1½ minutes, or until melted. Stir in crumbs until moistened. Press firmly and evenly against bottom and side of pie plate. Microwave at High 1 to 1½ minutes, or until set, rotating ½ turn after 1 minute. Cool.

In 3-qt. bowl mix brown sugar, ginger, nutmeg, cinnamon, salt, pumpkin and bitters. Place ice cream in medium bowl. Reduce power to 50% (Medium). Microwave 10 to 20 seconds, or until softened; stir. Fold into pumpkin mixture. Add pecans. Fold in whipped topping. Pour into cooled pie shell. Freeze at least 6 hours or overnight.

Mincemeat Pie ▼
Christmas Day, page 74

- 1 microwaved Whole Wheat Pastry Shell With Cut-Outs, page 139
- 1 pkg. (9 oz.) condensed mincemeat
- 1¼ cups water
- 1½ cups chopped apple
- ¾ cup raisins
- 2 tablespoons packed brown sugar
- 2 tablespoons brandy
- 1 tablespoon butter or margarine
- 1 teaspoon grated orange peel

Makes one 9-in. pie

Prepare Whole Wheat Pastry Shell With Cut-Outs. Crumble mincemeat into 4-cup measure or bowl. Add water. Microwave at High 6 to 7 minutes, or until water is absorbed, stirring after half the cooking time.

Mix in remaining ingredients. Pour into pastry shell. Set on wax paper in oven. Microwave at High 14 to 16 minutes, or until apples are tender and filling is hot and bubbly, rotating ¼ turn every 3 minutes. Cool. Arrange cut-outs on pie.

Chocolate Cake
Freezer Impromptu Dinner, page 28

- ⅓ cup all-purpose flour
- ⅓ cup sugar
- 2 tablespoons cocoa
- ½ teaspoon baking soda
- ⅛ teaspoon salt
- ¼ cup vegetable oil
- 2 tablespoons milk
- 1 egg
- ½ teaspoon vanilla
- Chocolate Frosting, below

Serves 2

Line bottoms only of two 12-oz. custard cups with wax paper. Mix all ingredients except frosting in small bowl. Divide batter equally between cups. Microwave at 50% (Medium) 3 minutes, rearranging cups once. Increase power to High. Microwave 30 seconds to 2 minutes, or until top springs back when touched, rearranging once. If one layer is done before the other, remove it from oven. Let stand on counter 5 minutes. Remove from cups. Cool on wire rack. Wrap, label and freeze up to 6 weeks.

To serve, unwrap layers and place on paper towel-lined plate. Microwave at 50% (Medium) 2 to 6 minutes, or until wooden pick inserted in center meets little or no resistance, rearranging once. Let stand while preparing frosting.

Place one layer on plate. Spread with one-fourth of the frosting. Place second layer on top. Frost side and top. Garnish, if desired.

Chocolate Frosting

- 1½ cups powdered sugar
- 1 tablespoon plus 1 teaspoon cocoa
- Dash salt
- 3 tablespoons butter or margarine, softened
- ¼ teaspoon vanilla
- 3 to 5 teaspoons milk

Frosts 2 small layers

In deep bowl mix sugar, cocoa, salt, butter and vanilla. Stir in milk, 1 teaspoon at a time, until frosting is spreading consistency.

Black Forest Cake

Dinner Party for Eight, page 16

Cake:
1¾ cups frozen, pitted dark
   sweet cherries, divided
¾ cup all-purpose flour
⅔ cup sugar
½ teaspoon baking soda
½ teaspoon salt
½ teaspoon vanilla

1 square (1 oz.) unsweetened
   chocolate, melted
⅓ cup shortening
⅓ cup milk
2 eggs

Cherry Filling:
¼ cup water
2 tablespoons Kirsch
2 teaspoons cornstarch

2 teaspoons sugar
2 to 3 drops red food coloring

Whipped Cream Mixture:
1 pint (2 cups) chilled
   whipping cream
¼ cup Kirsch

1 square (1 oz.) semi-sweet
   chocolate, optional

Makes 9-in. round cake

How to Microwave Black Forest Cake

Place cherries in 1-qt. casserole. Microwave at 50% (Medium) 2½ to 5 minutes, or until defrosted, stirring twice. Drain and chop. Line bottom of 9-in. round cake dish with circle of wax paper. Place all cake ingredients except cherries and 1 egg in large bowl.

Blend at low speed, then beat at medium speed 1 minute, scraping bowl constantly. Add remaining egg. Beat at high speed 1 minute, scraping bowl occasionally. Fold in two-thirds of the cherries. Spread in 9-in. round cake dish.

Place on inverted saucer in oven. Microwave at 50% (Medium) 6 minutes, rotating ¼ turn every 3 minutes. Increase power to High. Microwave 4 to 7 minutes, or until wooden pick inserted in center comes out clean. Let stand directly on counter 5 minutes.

Invert cake onto serving plate. Refrigerate until completely cool. Slice lengthwise to make 2 layers. Set aside. In small bowl combine remaining cherries and filling ingredients. Microwave at High 1 to 2 minutes, or until clear and thickened, stirring twice. Set aside.

Beat whipping cream in large, chilled bowl at high speed until slightly thickened. Add Kirsch, 1 tablespoon at a time, beating until thickened. Spread bottom layer of cake with one-third whipped cream mixture.

Spread cherry filling gently over whipped cream. Top with remaining layer. Frost top and side of cake with remaining whipped cream. Place semi-sweet chocolate in small bowl. Microwave at High 1½ to 2 minutes, or until melted. Drizzle over cake.

Apple Cake ▶

Labor Day, page 62

1½ cups all-purpose flour
1¼ cups packed brown sugar
1½ teaspoons baking powder
1½ teaspoons ground
    cinnamon
 1 teaspoon baking soda
¼ teaspoon ground nutmeg
¼ teaspoon ground cloves
 2 cups peeled, finely
    shredded apple
¾ cup vegetable oil
 4 eggs
¼ cup finely chopped nuts
    Honey Frosting, below

Makes two 8 × 8-in. cakes

Place all ingredients except Honey Frosting in large bowl. Blend at low speed, scraping bowl constantly. Beat at medium speed 2 minutes, scraping bowl occasionally. Divide batter between two 8 × 8-in. baking dishes.

Place one dish at a time on inverted saucer in oven. Microwave at 50% (Medium) 6 minutes, rotating ¼ turn every 3 minutes. Increase power to High. Microwave 1 to 4 minutes, or until top springs back when touched lightly. Let stand directly on counter 5 to 10 minutes. Cool and frost.

Honey Frosting

½ cup packed brown sugar
½ cup butter or margarine
½ cup honey
 4 cups powdered sugar
 2 teaspoons vanilla
 1 to 2 tablespoons milk

Frosts two 8 × 8-in. cakes

In medium bowl combine brown sugar, butter and honey. Micro-wave at High 2 to 3 minutes, or until boiling, stirring after half the time. Boil 30 seconds longer.

Stir in powdered sugar and vanilla. Add milk, 1 tablespoon at a time, beating until smooth and of spreading consistency. Cool before serving.

Honey Cake

Foreign Affair: East Indian, page 42

Cake:
 3 eggs, separated
⅓ cup honey
 3 tablespoons packed brown
    sugar
 2 tablespoons vegetable oil
 1 tablespoon water
 1 tablespoon grated orange
    peel
 1 teaspoon grated lemon peel
¾ cup all-purpose flour
 1 teaspoon ground cinnamon
 1 teaspoon ground allspice
¾ teaspoon baking powder
½ teaspoon ground cloves
¼ teaspoon baking soda
⅛ teaspoon salt

Topping:
⅓ cup honey
¼ cup butter or margarine
 1 tablespoon plus 1 teaspoon
    packed brown sugar
⅓ cup sliced almonds

Makes 1 cake

In deep bowl beat egg whites until stiff peaks form. In medium bowl beat egg yolks until frothy. Add honey, brown sugar, oil, water, orange peel and lemon peel. Beat until well blended. Mix in flour, cinnamon, allspice, baking powder, cloves, baking soda and salt. Fold batter into egg whites.

Pour into 8 × 5-in. loaf dish. Shield ends with foil. Place on inverted saucer in oven. Microwave at 50% (Medium) 3 minutes, rotating once. Remove shields. Microwave at 50% (Medium) 1 to 4 minutes, or until top springs back when lightly touched, rotating once or twice. Let stand on counter 5 minutes. Invert onto serving plate.

In small bowl or 2-cup measure combine topping ingredients except almonds. Microwave at High 1 to 4 minutes, or until butter melts, stirring once or twice. Stir to blend. Pierce top of cake with fork. Pour two-thirds of glaze slowly over cake. Sprinkle with almonds. Pour remaining glaze over cake.

Advance preparation: Honey Cake can be prepared 2 to 3 weeks in advance. Prepare cake as directed. Remove from pan but do not glaze; cool. Wrap, label and freeze no longer than 3 weeks. To serve, unwrap and place on serving plate. Microwave at 50% (Medium) 2 to 4 minutes, or until cake is defrosted and warm. Prepare glaze. Pour over cake as directed.

Festive Gelatin Cake ▲
Fourth of July, page 60

2 cups all-purpose flour
1¼ cups sugar
1 tablespoon baking powder
1 teaspoon salt
1 teaspoon vanilla
⅔ cup shortening
⅔ cup milk

2 eggs
4 egg whites
1 cup water
1 pkg. (3 oz.) gelatin, any
flavor
Fluffy Frosting, below

Makes two 8 × 8-in. cakes

Place all ingredients except water, gelatin and frosting in large bowl. Blend at low speed, scraping bowl constantly. Beat 2 minutes at medium speed, scraping bowl occasionally. Divide batter between two 8 × 8-in. baking dishes.

Microwave one dish at a time at 50% (Medium) 6 minutes, rotating twice. Increase power to High. Microwave 1 to 5 minutes or until top springs back when touched lightly. Let stand 10 minutes.

In 2-cup measure microwave water at High 1 to 3 minutes, or until boiling. Slowly add gelatin, stirring constantly. Pierce cakes at ¼-in. intervals with wooden pick. Pour half of gelatin mixture over each cake; cool. Frost with Fluffy Frosting. Refrigerate.

Fluffy Frosting

1 cup sugar
⅓ cup water
¼ teaspoon cream of tartar

⅛ teaspoon salt
2 egg whites
1 teaspoon vanilla

Frosts two 8 × 8-in. cakes

In 2-qt. casserole combine sugar, water, cream of tartar and salt; cover. Microwave at High 2 minutes. Stir. Microwave at High, uncovered, 1½ to 5 minutes, or until soft ball forms when small amount is dropped in cold water. Do not undercook.

Beat egg whites until stiff peaks form. Pour hot syrup slowly in a thin stream into beaten egg whites, beating constantly, until stiff and glossy. Add vanilla during last minute of beating.

Lemon Ring Cake
New Year's Eve, page 46

3 tablespoons graham
cracker crumbs
2 cups all-purpose flour
1¼ cups sugar
2 teaspoons baking powder
1 teaspoon salt
4 eggs
⅔ cup shortening
½ cup milk
1 tablespoon grated lemon
peel
1 teaspoon vanilla
4 drops yellow food coloring
¼ cup lemon juice
Lemon Glaze, below

Makes 1 ring cake

Grease 10- or 12-cup ring cake dish. Coat with graham cracker crumbs. Place all ingredients except lemon juice and glaze in medium bowl. Blend at low speed of electric mixer 30 seconds, scraping bowl constantly. Add lemon juice. Beat at medium speed 2 minutes, scraping bowl occasionally. Spread in dish.

Microwave at 50% (Medium) 8 minutes, rotating ¼ turn every 2 minutes. Increase power to High. Microwave 3 to 8 minutes, or until wooden pick inserted in several places comes out clean, rotating 2 or 3 times during cooking. Let stand directly on counter 5 to 10 minutes. Remove from pan to cool. Drizzle with Lemon Glaze.

Lemon Glaze

1¼ cups powdered sugar
1 teaspoon grated lemon peel
2 tablespoons lemon juice
1 tablespoon butter or
margarine
2 drops yellow food coloring

Frosts 1 ring cake

In medium bowl mix all ingredients until smooth.

Easter Cake

Easter, page 54

        1 pkg. (2-layer size) cake mix,
            any flavor
        Creamy Frosting, below
    1½ cups shredded coconut,
            divided
        2 drops green food coloring
        ½ teaspoon water
            Jelly beans

                Makes one 2-layer cake

Line the bottoms of two 8- or 9-in. round cake dishes with a circle of wax paper. Prepare cake mix as directed on package. Divide batter evenly between dishes.

Microwave one layer at a time at 50% (Medium) 5 minutes. Increase power to High. Microwave 1 to 6 minutes, or until top springs back when touched lightly, rotating dish 2 or 3 times. Let cake stand directly on counter 5 minutes. Remove from pan; cool. Repeat with remaining layer.

Fill and frost layers with Creamy Frosting. Sprinkle top and sides with 1 cup of the coconut. Place ½ cup coconut in jar or plastic bag. Mix in food coloring and water. Seal jar or bag; shake until coconut is evenly colored. Spoon coconut on top of cake in shape of nest. Place jelly beans inside.

Advance preparation: Prepare cake the day before. Cover loosely with foil taking care not to touch frosting.

Creamy Frosting

    ¼ cup plus 2 tablespoons
        butter or margarine
    ½ teaspon vanilla
    3 cups powdered sugar
    3 to 4 tablespoons half and half

In large bowl, beat butter and vanilla until blended. Gradually add sugar, beating at medium-high speed of electric mixer until blended. Add half and half, 1 tablespoon at a time, blending with electric mixer until frosting is desired consistency.

Petits Fours

Spring Open House, page 20

    1 pkg. (2-layer size) white   Petits Fours Icing,
        cake mix   below
    ½ teaspoon almond extract
                                                Makes 50

Prepare cake as directed on package adding almond extract with the water. Divide batter between two 8 × 8-in. baking dishes. Microwave one at a time at 50% (Medium) 6 minutes; rotate. Increase power to High. Microwave 1 to 3 minutes, or until cake pulls away from side and wooden pick inserted in center comes out clean. Let stand directly on counter 5 minutes. Remove from pan; cool on wire rack. Trim edges from cooled cake. Cut each into 1½-in. squares or diamonds.

Place one-third of cake pieces, with space between sides, on wire rack over baking sheet. Spoon green icing evenly over top and sides until completely covered. If necessary frost sides with metal spatula. Let icing dry. Spoon on second coat. Let dry. Repeat with white and pink icing, using one-third of the cake pieces for each color. Decorate with frosting flowers or whole almonds, if desired.

Petits Fours Icing

    3 cups granulated sugar   1 cup powdered sugar
    ¼ teaspoon cream of tartar   1 drop red food coloring
    1½ cups hot water   1 drop green food coloring
    1 teaspoon vanilla or almond
        extract

                                Frosts 50 Petits Fours

In 3-qt. mixing bowl combine granulated sugar, cream of tartar and water; cover. Microwave at High 6 to 8 minutes, or until just boiling. Uncover. Microwave at High 10 to 15 minutes or until mixture reaches 226°F. on candy thermometer. Let stand on counter until cooled to 110°F. (Do not stir or cool over ice water.) Stir in vanilla and powdered sugar until icing is of pouring consistency and smooth. Divide among 3 bowls. Mix green food coloring into one, red food coloring into another and leave one white.

Pound Cake & Strawberries

Freezer Buffet, page 36

    2 to 3 tablespoons sugar   2 pkgs. (10¾ oz. each) frozen
    1½ qts. fresh strawberries,   loaf pound cakes
        hulled and halved   Sweetened whipped cream

                                        Serves 10 to 12

Sprinkle sugar over fresh strawberries. Let stand several hours.

Place each unwrapped cake on plate. Microwave one at 70% (Medium-High) 45 seconds to 1½ minutes, or until wooden pick inserted in center meets no resistance. Let stand 5 minutes. Repeat with remaining cake. Cut cakes into ¾-in. slices, then cut slices into halves or thirds. Serve with strawberries and sweetened whipped cream.

Variation:
Substitute 3 pkgs. (10 oz. each) frozen sliced strawberries, defrosted, for the fresh strawberries. Omit sugar.

Ice Cream-Filled Cake

Adult Birthday Party, page 24

2 tablespoons sugar
1 pkg. (2-layer size) chocolate
    cake mix
1 qt. peppermint ice cream
½ cup chocolate chips
½ cup corn syrup
1 tablespoon half and half
½ teaspoon vanilla

Makes 1 ring cake

How to Microwave Ice Cream-Filled Cake

Grease 12- to 14-cup ring cake dish. Sprinkle with sugar. Prepare cake mix as directed on package. Pour into dish. Microwave at 50% (Medium) 12 minutes, rotating every 4 minutes. Increase power to High.

Microwave 4 to 7 minutes, or until cake begins to pull away from side. Let stand 10 minutes. Carefully loosen edges; invert on wire rack to cool.

Cut off top quarter of cooled cake; set aside. Remove center of cake by cutting ½ inch from inner and outer edge to within 1 inch from bottom.

Scoop out inside with spoon leaving 1 inch of cake on bottom. Refigerate or freeze at least 1 hour.

Place ice cream in medium bowl. Microwave at 30% (Medium-Low) 30 to 60 seconds, or until softened. Spoon into cake. Replace top. Freeze at least 6 hours.

Combine chocolate chips and syrup in 1-qt. casserole. Microwave at High 30 to 60 seconds, or until chips melt. Stir in half and half and vanilla. Pour over cake before serving.

Almond Cheesecake

Freezer Dinner, page 30

Crust:

1 tablespoon butter or
   margarine
¼ cup graham cracker crumbs
1 teaspoon granulated sugar
½ teaspoon packed brown
   sugar

Filling:

1 pkg. (3 oz.) cream cheese
3 tablespoons granulated
   sugar
1 egg
   Dash salt
¼ teaspoon almond extract

Topping:

¼ cup dairy sour cream
2 teaspoons packed brown
   sugar
1 to 2 drops almond extract

Serves 2

Melt butter in small bowl at High 30 to 60 seconds. Mix in remaining crust ingredients until blended. Press half in bottom of each of two 6-oz. custard cups. Microwave both at High 30 seconds to 1½ minutes, or until set. Set aside.

In small bowl blend cream cheese and 3 tablespoons sugar. Mix in remaining filling ingredients. Reduce power to 50% (Medium). Microwave 1½ to 3½ minutes, or until thickened, blending with wire whip every 30 to 45 seconds. Pour half into each custard cup. Chill at least 2 hours.

Blend all topping ingredients. Spread over chilled cheesecakes. Sprinkle with sliced almonds, if desired.

Advance preparation:

Cheesecakes can be wrapped and frozen in the custard cups no longer than 2 weeks. To defrost, unwrap and microwave at 50% (Medium) 1 to 3 minutes, or until wooden pick inserted in the center meets little or no resistance, checking frequently.

Sesame Bars

Holiday Make-Aheads, page 69

1 cup packed brown sugar
⅓ cup butter or margarine
1 cup sesame seed
½ cup all-purpose flour
½ teaspoon salt
1 egg
½ teaspoon vanilla

Makes 25

In medium bowl beat brown sugar and butter until creamy. Beat in sesame seed, flour, salt, egg and vanilla. Spread in 8 × 8-in. baking dish. Shield corners with foil. Place on inverted saucer in oven. Microwave at 70% (Medium-High) 8 to 11 minutes, or until edges just begin to pull away from sides and no uncooked batter can be seen on bottom, rotating 2 or 3 times. (Bars will appear foamy on top.) Let stand directly on counter 10 minutes. Cut into about 1½-in. squares. Store at room temperature, tightly covered, no longer than 2 weeks.

Fruitcake Cookies

Holiday Make-Aheads, page 69

¾ cup packed dark brown
   sugar
⅓ cup butter or margarine
1¼ cups all-purpose flour
½ teaspoon baking soda
½ teaspoon salt

1 egg
2 tablespoons rum
2 cups chopped candied
   fruits
1 cup chopped dates
1 cup chopped nuts

Makes 4½ dozen

In medium bowl beat brown sugar and butter until creamy. Mix in flour, baking soda, salt, egg and rum. Spread in 8 × 8-in. baking dish. Stir in candied fruits, dates and nuts. Shape into two 12- to 13-in. long rolls on plastic wrap. Wrap and refrigerate overnight, or until well chilled. Cut into ½-in. slices. Place 8 slices in circle near edge on large plate.

Microwave at 50% (Medium) 1½ to 4½ minutes, or until center surface is just dry, rotating plate once or twice. Let stand 1 minute. Cool on rack or paper towel. Repeat with remaining slices, 8 at a time. Store at room temperature, tightly covered, no longer than 3 weeks.

Molasses Cookies

Halloween, page 64

¾ cup packed brown sugar
¾ cup shortening
¼ cup molasses
1 egg
1½ teaspoons baking soda
1 teaspoon ground cinnamon
1 teaspoon ground ginger
½ teaspoon ground cloves
¼ teaspoon salt
2⅓ cups all-purpose flour
   Granulated sugar

Makes 3 dozen

Place all ingredients except flour and granulated sugar in large bowl. Beat until light and fluffy. Mix in flour. Chill 1 hour.

Shape dough into 1-in. balls. Place 6 to 8 in large ring on wax paper. Microwave at 50% (Medium) 1½ to 4 minutes, or just until surface is dry, rotating 2 or 3 times during cooking. Remove wax paper with cookies to counter. Sprinkle cookies with sugar while still warm. Repeat with remaining cookies.

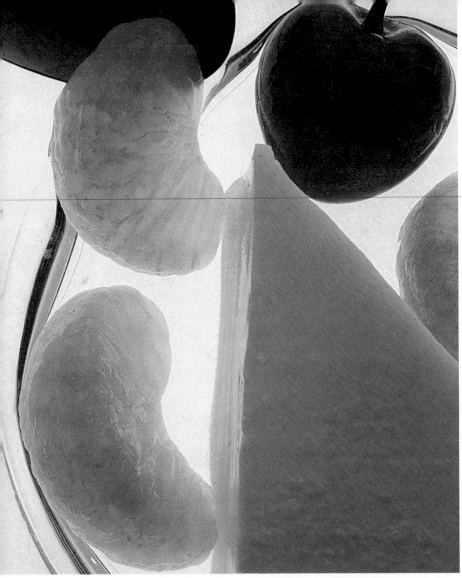

◀ Floating Almond Dessert

Foreign Affair: Oriental, page 38

Gelatin:

1 envelope unflavored gelatin
2 cups milk, divided
¼ cup plus 2 tablespoons
    sugar
1 tablespoon almond extract

Sauce:

¼ cup sugar
½ cup warm water
1 cup cold water
1 can (11 oz.) mandarin
    orange sections, drained
    and juice reserved
1 teaspoon almond extract
8 maraschino cherries

Serves 8

Advance preparation: Gelatin
and sauce can be prepared
several days in advance and
refrigerated. Assemble just
before serving.

How to Microwave Floating Almond Dessert

Stir gelatin into ¾ cup of the
milk in small bowl. In medium
bowl or 1½-qt. casserole
combine remaining 1¼ cups
milk and ¼ cup plus 2
tablespoons sugar. Microwave
at High 2 to 5 minutes, or until
heated but not boiling. Blend in
gelatin and almond extract.

Pour into 8 × 5-in. loaf dish.
Refrigerate overnight, or until
set. To prepare sauce, stir ¼
cup sugar and the warm water
until sugar dissolves. Mix in
cold water, reserved juice and
almond extract.

Cut gelatin into 16 triangles.
Place 2 triangles in each of 8
dessert dishes and divide
sauce equally among dishes.
Garnish with mandarin orange
sections and cherries.

Dickens' Plum Pudding

Christmas Eve, page 72

2 tablespoons granulated
    sugar
4 cups soft white bread cubes
1 cup all-purpose flour
¼ cup packed brown sugar
1 teaspoon baking soda
1 teaspoon ground cinnamon
¼ teaspoon salt
¼ teaspoon ground nutmeg
¾ cup orange juice
½ cup butter or margarine,
    softened
⅓ cup brandy
3 tablespoons dark molasses
2 eggs
1 teaspoon grated lemon peel
¾ cup raisins
½ cup currants
    Hard Sauce, below

Serves 6 to 8

Generously grease 8-cup ring
baking dish. Coat bottom and
side with granulated sugar.
Place remaining ingredients
except Hard Sauce in large
bowl. Beat at medium speed of
electric mixer 2 minutes, or until
blended, scraping bowl
occasionally. Spoon into dish.
Cover with plastic wrap. Place
on inverted saucer in oven.

Microwave at 50% (Medium) 12
to 17 minutes, or until pudding
pulls away from edge of dish
and wooden pick inserted in
center comes out clean. Let
stand, covered, 5 minutes.
Invert onto serving dish. Serve
warm with Hard Sauce.

Hard Sauce

½ cup butter or margarine
2 cups powdered sugar
2 tablespoons water
2 teaspoons grated orange
    peel

Makes about 2 cups

Beat butter at high speed of
electric mixer until fluffy. Mix
in remaining ingredients.

Mocha Pudding ▶

Simple Dinner for Four, page 14

¾ cup sugar
⅓ cup cocoa
3 tablespoons cornstarch
2 teaspoons instant coffee
    crystals
¼ teaspoon salt
1½ cups milk
½ cup coffee liqueur
3 egg yolks, beaten
⅓ cup whipped cream or
    prepared whipped topping
1 teaspoon coffee liqueur or
    chocolate syrup

Serves 4

In 2-qt. casserole mix sugar,
cocoa, cornstarch, instant
coffee and salt. Blend in milk
and ½ cup coffee liqueur.
Microwave at High 4 to 7
minutes, or until thick, stirring
with wire whip once or twice.

Blend in egg yolks. Microwave
at High 1 minute. Stir with wire
whip. Pour into 4 individual
dishes. Place plastic wrap
directly on surface of each
pudding. Chill several hours or
overnight, or serve warm.
Before serving, blend whipped
cream and 1 teaspoon coffee
liqueur in small bowl. Spoon
equally onto puddings.

Variation:
Substitute ½ cup milk for coffee
liqueur in pudding.

Mexican Sundaes

After the Game, page 22

2 jars (12 oz. each) chocolate
    fudge topping
½ teaspoon ground cinnamon
½ teaspoon ground nutmeg
2 qts. ice cream

Serves 10 to 12

In small bowl mix topping,
cinnamon and nutmeg.
Microwave at 50% (Medium)
1½ to 3 minutes, or until
heated, stirring once or twice.
Serve over ice cream.

Chocolate Amaretto Sauce

Freezer Dinner, page 34

⅔ cup granulated sugar
⅔ cup packed brown sugar
3 tablespoons all-purpose flour
¼ cup cocoa
    Dash salt
1 cup Amaretto
¼ cup butter or margarine
1 tablespoon corn syrup

Makes about 1½ cups

In medium bowl or 1½-qt.
casserole mix sugars, flour,
cocoa and salt. Stir in remaining
ingredients. Microwave at High
7 to 8 minutes, or until thick and
smooth, stirring once or twice.
Serve over spumoni ice cream,
if desired.

Advance preparation: Prepare
sauce; cover and refrigerate no
longer than 1 week. To reheat,
microwave at High 2 to 5
minutes, or until heated and
smooth, stirring once or twice
with wire whip.

Candies

Popcorn Balls
Halloween, page 64

2⅔ cups sugar
1½ cups hot water
⅔ cup dark corn syrup
2 teaspoons vinegar
2 teaspoons vanilla
12 cups popped popcorn

Makes 12

Advance preparation: Can be made 2 to 3 days in advance.

Caramel Apples pictured at left
Halloween, page 64

12 medium red Delicious or
    McIntosh apples
12 wooden sticks
 2 pkgs. (14 oz. each)
    caramels

¼ cup half and half
½ cup chocolate-flavored or
    colored candy sprinkles

Makes 12

Wash and dry apples. Insert sticks in stem ends. Place caramels and half and half in 2-qt. casserole. Microwave at High 4 to 7 minutes, or until melted, stirring every minute.

Dip each apple in hot caramel until coated. Coat bottoms with candy sprinkles. Cool apples on wax paper.

How to Microwave Popcorn Balls

Combine sugar, hot water, corn syrup and vinegar in 3-qt. casserole.

Microwave at High 35 to 40 minutes, or until hard crack stage (300° to 310°F.), when syrup separates into hard, brittle threads when small amount is dropped into cold water, stirring 3 or 4 times.

Stir in vanilla. Pour syrup over popcorn, stirring to coat. Quickly shape into balls, using buttered hands.

Place on wax paper; cool completely. Wrap each in plastic wrap.

Chocolate Covered ▲ Marshmallows

Halloween, page 64
Holiday Make-Aheads, page 69

1 cup chocolate chips
¼ cup shortening
2 cups chopped nuts
1 pkg. (10 oz.) large
   marshmallows
50 wooden picks

Makes 50

Place chocolate chips and shortening in 2-cup measure. Microwave at 50% (Medium) 1½ to 3½ minutes, or until chips are shiny and soft. Stir until smooth.

Place nuts in shallow dish. Insert pick in top of each marshmallow. Dip in chocolate to cover completely. Roll in nuts, coating about three-fourths the way up. Set on wax paper. Repeat with remaining marsh-mallows. Let stand until firm. Stir together leftover nuts and chocolate. Drop by spoonfuls onto wax paper. Wrap marshmallows and candy drops individually in plastic wrap or store in covered container.

Buttermilk Pralines ▲

Holiday Make-Aheads, page 69

2 cups sugar
1 teaspoon baking soda
1 cup buttermilk
¾ cup butter or margarine
1 teaspoon vanilla
2 cups pecan halves

Makes 4 dozen

Butter 3-qt. mixing bowl. Stir in sugar, baking soda, buttermilk and butter. Microwave at 50% (Medium) 30 to 40 minutes, or until a soft ball forms in cold water, stirring 2 or 3 times during cooking. Add vanilla. Beat at high speed of electric mixer until soft peaks form. Stir in pecans.

Drop by teaspoonfuls onto wax paper. Cool until firm. Store in tightly covered container in freezer no longer than 3 months or in refrigerator no longer than 1½ months.

Chocolate Bourbon Balls ▲

Holiday Make-Aheads, page 69

1½ cups fine vanilla wafer
   crumbs
⅓ cup bourbon
1 cup semi-sweet chocolate
   chips
2 tablespoons butter or
   margarine
½ cup finely chopped pecans
1¼ to 1½ cups powdered
   sugar, divided

Makes 4 dozen

In small bowl mix cookie crumbs and bourbon. Set aside. Place chips and butter in large bowl. Microwave at 50% (Medium) 2 to 5 minutes, or until chips are soft. Stir until smooth. Stir in pecans and crumb mixture. Gradually mix in enough sugar until mixture just holds together. Shape by teaspoonfuls into balls; place on wax paper. Roll in remaining sugar to coat. Store in refrigerator, tightly covered, no longer than 2 weeks.

Coconut Date Balls ▲
Holiday Make-Aheads, page 69

2 cups chopped dates
¾ cup sugar
½ cup butter or margarine
1 egg
2 tablespoons milk
1 teaspoon vanilla
½ teaspoon salt
2 cups crushed corn flakes
½ cup chopped pecans
1 cup flaked coconut

Makes 5½ dozen

In medium bowl combine dates, sugar and butter. Microwave at High 4 minutes, stirring 2 or 3 times. Stir until all butter is absorbed. In small bowl mix egg, milk, vanilla and salt. Stir a small amount of hot dates into egg mixture, then return to dates, stirring constantly.

Reduce power to 50% (Medium). Microwave 5 to 8 minutes, or until thickened and mixture forms a ball when stirred. Mix in corn flakes and pecans. Shape into 1-in. balls; roll in coconut. Place on wax paper. Chill until set. Store in refrigerator or at room temperature, tightly covered, no longer than 2 weeks.

Apricot Chews ▲
New Year's Day, page 48

½ cup butter or margarine
1 cup granulated sugar
⅓ cup all-purpose flour
½ teaspoon salt
2 eggs
1 cup chopped dried apricots
3 cups wheat flake cereal, coarsely crushed
1 cup chopped pecans
1 teaspoon vanilla
½ to ¾ cup powdered sugar

Makes 4½ dozen

Place butter in 2-qt. bowl or casserole. Microwave at High 45 seconds to 1¼ minutes, or until melted. Blend in granulated sugar, flour, salt and eggs. Stir in apricots. Microwave at High 3½ to 6 minutes, or until very thick, stirring every 2 minutes. Cool 5 minutes.

In large bowl, combine cereal and pecans. Stir in apricot mixture and vanilla until all ingredients are well distributed. Shape into 1-in. balls. Place powdered sugar in plastic bag. Shake a few apricot balls at a time in bag until coated. Repeat. Refrigerate 2 to 3 hours, or until chilled.

Thin Mint Layers ▲
Holiday Make-Aheads, page 69

1 pkg. (6 oz.) semi-sweet chocolate chips
3 tablespoons butter or margarine, divided
1 cup powdered sugar
⅛ teaspoon peppermint extract
2 to 5 drops green food coloring
3 to 4 teaspoons milk

Makes 25

In 2-cup measure combine chocolate chips and 2 tablespoons butter. Microwave at High 45 seconds to 1½ minutes, or until chips are soft. Stir until smooth. Spread in 8 × 8-in. baking dish. Chill about 1 hour, or until set.

In medium bowl combine sugar, 1 tablespoon butter, the peppermint extract and food coloring. Beat with electric mixer, adding milk as needed, until smooth and stiff frosting consistency. Spread on chilled chocolate layer. Chill 3 to 4 hours, or until firm. Cut into about 1½-in. squares. Store in refrigerator, tightly covered, no longer than 1 week.

Index